PHILADELPHIA'S
KING of LITTLE ITALY

PHILADELPHIA'S KING of LITTLE ITALY

C.C.A. BALDI & HIS BROTHERS

CHARLES G. DOUGLAS, III

WITH VICTOR L. BALDI, III, AND DOUGLAS BALDI SWIFT

THE
History
PRESS

Published by The History Press
Charleston, SC
www.historypress.com

Back cover, left: Photo of the editors of *L'Opinione. From Michael di Pilla,* South Philadelphia's Little Italy *(2016)*; *right*: The coal yard. *Victor Baldi Collection.*

First published 2022

Manufactured in the United States

ISBN 9781467150279

Library of Congress Control Number: 2022939451

C.C.A. Baldi with the medal he received as a chevalier, 1907. *Author's collection.*

CONTENTS

Contents

INTRODUCTION

This book is about a man I never met, yet always admired, from the stories told to me as a young boy growing up in the suburbs of Philadelphia. It is a collaboration of three cousins who want to share the life of a boy who came to America at the age of fourteen and started to earn money by selling lemons from a pushcart in Philadelphia. C.C.A. Baldi and his brothers came to the land of opportunity and succeeded in business. From publishing newspapers to both being born on December 2, C.C.A. and I share similarities that have led to a fascination for me that now can be shared with all.

My cousin Douglas Baldi Swift of Midland, Texas, did a massive amount of newspaper research on the internet that yielded hundreds of clippings over a fifty-year period from 1880 to 1930 about the Baldis. Cousin Victor L. Baldi, III of Philadelphia has supplied photographs from his family collection that help chronicle the Baldi brothers' story and is the fourth generation of Baldis to run the funeral home.

Skylar and Jennifer Jameson of Hillsborough, New Hampshire, typed the manuscript, and Denise Ehmling of Epsom, New Hampshire, did final revisions for publication. I appreciate all they did in translating my handwriting.

CHAPTER I

THE LAND LEFT BEHIND

The Mezzogiorno region of Italy is where the midday sun is hottest. Mountains and sheep, as well as poor peasants, made up the former kingdom of Naples. The regions of Abruzzi, Molise, Campania, Puglia, Basilicata and Calabria constitute the Mezzogiorno on the mainland. The Apennine Mountain Range takes up half the land area but is too steep to cultivate. Less than twenty inches of rain falls on the Mezzogiorno. Large estates dominated the region in the 1800s, and its educational level was the worst in Italy. In fact, around 1900, almost 64 percent of the Italians arriving in the United States were illiterate.[1]

C.C.A. Baldi's birthplace of Castelnuovo Cilento is in the foothills several miles inland from the Gulf of Salerno, and the largest city near the town is Salerno. Castelnuovo is part of the Parco Nazionale del Cilento, a national park in the province of Salerno in the region known as Campania in southern Italy. It is one of the largest national parks in Italy, at seven hundred square miles.

Castelnuovo is a town with a medieval castle and was part of the fief of the Agnello family. It lies on a hill above the Alento River. *Cilento* was added to the name in 1861, after the unification of Italy. The focal points are the castle and the Church of Santa Maria Maddalena, dedicated to Mary Magdalene. In more recent times, an artist and village character named Guerino Galzerano (1922–2002) built the House of Pebbles, which is a tourist attraction with two bedrooms rentable for short visits.

Top: Map of southern Italy. *Public domain.*

Middle: The castle in Castelnuovo Cilento. *Town website.*

Below: Church of Santa Maria Maddalena. *Town website.*

Top: Guerino Galzerano and his house of pebbles. *Wikimedia.*

Bottom: The town. *Town website.*

The Baldi and Galzerano families came together in Castelnuovo when Vito Baldi married Rosa Galzerano. She gave birth to Carmine (C.C.A.), Virgilio, Joseph, Guerino and Alfonso between 1862 and 1886: the five Baldi brothers. There was also one sister. Upon a return visit to Italy by C.C.A., the home was decorated with the flags of Italy and America.

It is not clear where Vito was born, but the historic center of gravity for the Baldis was in northern Italy. The surname Baldi was first found in the city of Cremona, south of Milan. *Baldi* is derived from the Germanic word *baltha*, which means "gallant" or "bold." The use of surnames in addition to first names began in Italy only in the tenth and eleventh centuries.

Vito and Rosa in 1881. *Author's collection.*

Baldi house in Castelnuovo Cilento in the 1920s. *Giuseppe Galzerano Collection.*

The Baldi Crest

Italian towns were largely farming communities, with the fields below the village on a hill. The bulk of southern Italians were *contadini*, or agricultural workers.

> *These peasants were not from rurally isolated farms however, they were town dwellers who owned, or leased, and worked small parcels of land. Landless peasants who journeyed daily to places of agricultural labor were called* giornalieri *or day workers. Dominated physically and psychologically for centuries by a massive feudal structure, the* contadini *and* giornalieri *were minimally affected by the sudden abolition of feudalism. In fact, the lives of all poverty-ridden southern Italians remained essentially unaltered. Land tenure continued to be insecure and uncertain.*[2]

There was no strong middle class, but in the social pecking order above the *contadini* were artisans such as tailors, shoemakers and other skilled craftsmen, as well as small shopkeepers.[3] The occupation of Vito Baldi remains a mystery; however, he came to America with his sons Carmine and Virgilio in 1876. They did not come as contract labor, so they must have had the funds for three of them to come over. Later, the Baldis were joined by Giuseppe Fioravanti, the third-born brother. Records show the third-youngest brother, born in 1870, was Joseph or Giuseppe, who named his son Joseph F.M. (Fioravanti Menotti) Baldi upon the boy's birth in 1894.

Baldi crest. *Robert Baldi Collection.*

When they came to America, Italy had been united just a few years before in what was known as the Risorgimento. The Risorgimento was the name of the movement to free the Italian city states and principalities from foreign control and unite them in one kingdom of Italy. The first king was Victor Emmanuel, II, who died in 1878. His son, Victor Emmanuel, III (ruled 1900–46), would later decorate C.C.A. Baldi and make him a cavalier, or knight, as well as a commendatore. The military leader of the Risorgimento was Giuseppe Garibaldi, who brought Naples and Sicily into the kingdom.

King Victor Emmanuel,
III. *Wikipedia.*

Following Italy in unification was the consolidation of German states into one empire in 1871 under Otto von Bismarck as its first chancellor. One month after the chancellor's death (July 30, 1898), C.C.A.'s wife, Louise (whose parents were German), gave birth to a son on August 31, 1898. He was named Virgil Bismark Baldi in honor of the great German unifier.

Unfortunately, after the Italian unification, harsh taxes were imposed on the southern Italians up to a rate of 30 percent.[4] This accelerated an exodus to the United States. Also, in 1864, President Lincoln welcomed Europeans to come to our shores with his Act to Encourage Immigration to help fill the Union ranks with more soldiers.

CHAPTER 2

PHILADELPHIA AND THE ITALIANS

The earliest contacts between the Philadelphia area and Italy occurred during the seventeenth century. A handful of Waldensians—members of a Christian but non-Catholic movement—reportedly landed at New Castle (later included in Delaware) in 1665 to escape religious persecution in their native Piedmont. "Both William Penn (1644–1718) and Francis Daniel Pastorius (1615–1720), the founder of Germantown, visited Italy and learned the language. Penn's successors built on Pennsylvania's record of freedom of conscience and self-government to lure prospective settlers from northern Italy."[5] The first Italian who spent time in Philadelphia was probably John Palma (Giovanni di Palma), a composer who directed a concert in the city in 1757. Other musicians followed, along with some artists, scientists, intellectuals, merchants, artisans, vendors of plaster statues and small entrepreneurs.[6] Although *The Directory of Philadelphia* in 1791 listed only nine residents with Italian-sounding last names, it likely missed those who had Americanized their surnames, as well as recent and temporary dwellers.

In 1791, the Republic of Genoa appointed the first consul in Philadelphia from the Italian peninsula to assume responsibility for trade relations.[7] During the first half of the nineteenth century, the Italian community grew slowly and contained mostly immigrants from Liguria and Tuscany. Many were political exiles.[8] They fled the northern regions of their motherland following the initial setbacks of the Risorgimento and went to the United States because independence had consolidated the nation's image as a model of liberty and free government.[9] In Italian eyes, Philadelphia, where the Declaration of Independence was signed and the federal Constitution was drafted, became the epitome of freedom.[10]

These early émigrés were skilled workers who quickly became fluent in English as they Americanized. As such, they were welcomed in Philadelphia and found opportunities to advocate and raise money for the cause of Italy's self-rule. Further enhancing the initial climate of favorable regard for Italy and its immigrants, a number of prominent local families included Italy in their "Grand Tours" of Europe.[11]

The contingent of Italians numbered only a few more than one hundred residents in 1852, when they succeeded in persuading Bishop John Neumann to have St. Mary Magdalen de Pazzi on Montrose Street established as the first Italian Catholic parish nationwide, with Gaetano Mariani as its pastor. Fifteen years later, the Società di Unione e Fratellanza Italiana opened its doors at 746 South Eighth Street as the city's first benevolent and fraternal Italian American ethnic association.[12] These two institutions offered the formal foundations for the subsequent development of an Italian community that, by 1870, comprised only 516 people located in a neighborhood bounded by Christian, Seventh, Carpenter and Ninth Streets in a South Philadelphia district where the price of real estate was lower than in other areas.[13]

By the 1880s, larger numbers of Italians were coming to Philadelphia for railroad track gang jobs and then laboring jobs due to the *padrone* system of labor, as described by Professor Luconi in his Encyclopedia of Greater Philadelphia:

> *While the city's economy diversified, Italians spread to other locations in the Pennsylvania suburbs and in many parts of southern New Jersey. By 2010, the U.S. Census identified the Philadelphia metropolitan region as home to the second-largest Italian-American population in the United States with about 3,100 Italian immigrants living in the city and more than 142,000 residents identifying as having Italian ancestry. Well beyond the iconic neighborhood of South Philadelphia with its Italian Market along Ninth Street, they sustained a presence in multiple forms and locations.*[14]

Michael Di Pilla writes in *South Philadelphia's Little Italy*:

> *Most Italians lived in South Philadelphia in the area centered on Eighth and Christian Streets. During this period, there were large concentrations from*

Italian outdoor market on South Ninth Street. *From Miller, Vogel and Davis,* Still Philadelphia *(1988).*

the provinces of Campobasso, Chieti, Salerno, Palermo, and Catanzaro. It is difficult to determine the exact number of Italians at the beginning of the 20th century. According to the locals, it would be impossible for the census to accurately determine the number of Italians in Philadelphia. Only a few spoke English. The majority of Italians came from Abruzzi (Molise and Abruzzo) and Sicily.... They lived in an area the Americans called "Little Italy." Early newspapers referred to the area as the Italian Quarter or the Italian Colony.[15]

The city's Italian-born population grew from 10,023 in 1890 to 136,793 in 1920, while their area of settlement in South Philadelphia extended north to Bainbridge Street and southwestward to Federal Street along Passyunk Avenue. Additional but smaller communities sprang up in Manayunk, Roxborough and elsewhere.[16]

The mushrooming of new Italian Catholic parishes offered further evidence of the creation and growth of these colonies. St. Lucy was founded in Manayunk in 1906, Our Lady of the Angels in West Philadelphia in 1907,

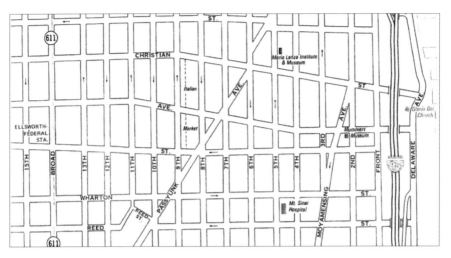

Italian section of South Philadelphia. *From* 1992 Visitors Guide to Philadelphia.

St. Donato in Overbook in 1910, Our Lady of the Rosary in Germantown in 1914 and Our Lady of Consolation in Frankford in 1917. By 1932, the Philadelphia Archdiocese included as many as twenty-three Italian parishes.[17]

The peak year for Italian immigration was 1906, when 358,000 Italians arrived in the United States. A quarter of them came from the Baldis' region of Campania.

C.C.A. BALDI'S START IN PHILADELPHIA

According to Frangini's 1907 book, *Italiani in Filadelfia*, C.C.A. attended Italian public schools and a private one as well. Frangini lists C.C.A.'s teachers as Alfonso Crisci, Ogliastro Cilento, Don Gaetano de Marino and John Calabria. According to Professor Richard Varbero, the firstborn child of Vito and Rosa earned money for his passage to America as a professional letter writer for folks in the area who had relatives in the States. In a short article in the *Reading Times* in 1919, C.C.A. himself said he started out with forty cents in his pocket. His talk in Reading was an admonishment to his fellow Italians "to be honest and upright in their dealings, and success would surely reward them."[18]

C.C.A.'s age upon arriving in America in 1876 or 1877 is listed as either fourteen or fifteen. Passenger lists for the ship SS *England*, arriving in New York in November 1877, listed Vito as being forty-one, Carmine as twelve and Virgil as ten. Listing the boys as younger than they actually were got them a discount on the price of the tickets. C.C.A.'s birth certificate is in the appendix.

However, a petition in the Court of Common Pleas for Philadelphia County seeking citizenship in 1884 recounted that C.C.A. arrived in the port of New York "in the year 1876, and that at the time of his arrival he was under eighteen years of age; that he has continued to reside in the United States since that period." His residence on September 4, 1884, was 319 Green Lane in Roxborough. Thanks to no computers back then, the court was not aware that C.C.A. had actually returned to Italy in the early 1880s and served in the Italian army for several months before returning to Philadelphia. His citizenship application is in the appendix.

What did C.C.A. do to earn money in Philadelphia? Stefano Luconi's book says that fifteen-year-old Carmine started out as a "lemon hawker." At some point, Carmine adopted the first name of Charles and then changed Carmine to Carmen for Charles Carmen Antonio Baldi, or C.C.A., as he became so widely known.

One version of the early days had C.C.A. hawking lemons as a *venditore ambulante* using a pushcart:

> *Subsequently Baldi cornered the market at 22nd and Spring Garden Streets; in league with his brothers Alphonse and Virgil, the business alternately thrived and sagged. C.C.A. Baldi left the United States during this time to fulfill his Italian military obligation; on his return he became a United States citizen and resumed his personal campaign for success.*[19]

Francini's book says the Baldis were fruit dealers, buying and selling consignments of fruit from a fruit shop. By 1879, they had moved to Atlantic City, New Jersey, but business got bad, and everyone went back to Italy. Shortly thereafter, the three Baldi brothers were back in Philadelphia, but in the interim, seventeen-year-old C.C.A. met his required military obligation by serving in the Italian army for less than a year. According to Francini, after a few months, his obligation ceased at Cava de Tirreni. That service as an Italian soldier would later be rewarded when Premier Benito Mussolini made him a commendatore in the Italian army.

A 1915 newspaper article gave much more detail on the lemon business, relating that C.C.A. had secured the lemon contract with most of city's hotels:

> *The cellar of the house then at 1003 South 8th street, was used as a headquarters, and he found it necessary to press his two younger brothers into service to help supply the trade. One day he bought every lemon in the city at the rate of $1.26 a box. Two or three days later the fruit jumped in value by leaps and bounds and the youthful lemon merchant sold the lemons at the rate of $7 and $8 a box.*

Then he and his brothers rented a stall in the farmers' market at 22nd and Spring Garden Streets, and this was the official start of C.C.A. Baldi & Brothers.[20]

WAS C.C.A. A PADRONE?

L uconi's Encyclopedia of Greater Philadelphia says that C.C.A. "became a sophisticated version of a *padrone* and recruited workers for railroad companies."[21] The *padrone* system arose in Italy after the unification of 1861, due to a lack of jobs in the south and not enough useful land for a growing population. *Padrone* means boss or manager who contracts to bring laborers from Italy to America in return for a cut or "tribute" of their earnings. Funds were advanced for the contract laborer to pay for his passage to America on a steamship from Italy.

Richard Varbero, in his 1975 work, devoted many pages to the *padrone* system, which generally had died out by 1911. The *padrone*

> *did provide concrete aid to immigrants, finding them jobs, housing, and other forms of sustenance during the difficult periods of adjustment. Generalizations about the* padrone, *then must be qualified, because no definite pattern predominated; the system was widespread and covered a variety of manual occupations. The* padrone *was evidently both exploiter and benefactor, his temperament and conscience determining how much of each he was. Bossism was a universal economic feature associated with many newly-arrived immigrant groups.*[22]

The *padroni* brought together American capital and Italian labor:

> *A number of these services were integral in the adjustment process, such as helping the immigrant collect his wages, writing letters for him, and advising him on banking and rent matters.*

The 1890s were a high point in the padrone *system, and its decline had begun at the time of the largest Italian immigration in 1914. By this date, the conditions and character of immigration had changed. Community stability and increased familiarity with the English language and American labor practices helped curtail the* padrone's *function.*[23]

C.C.A. combined the role of the *padrone* with that of ward boss for the Republican machine under Charles Vare. The Irish, Jews and other immigrant groups trended Democratic, so rather than be another group on that side of the aisle, C.C.A. cut a deal with Vare to get Italians jobs in return for delivering Republican votes from the fastest-growing ethnic group in the city. Varbero says that the one *padrone* who worked in league with the Republican machine as its ethnic intermediary was C.C.A., "thus giving him control over workers."[24]

As the political and economic boss, the relationship was very transactional—jobs for votes. Varbero describes it well:

They employed their effective ward organizations to expedite the naturalization process for newcomers and helped them establish social clubs. This by no means insulated or protected the workers from the Italian "bosses," but it brought Italian workers into the focus of the Vare machine, and as a result, employment opportunities were opened within the Vare brothers' street-cleaning and contracting businesses which were beyond the direct control of the padroni. *In Philadelphia, unskilled Italian workers staked an exclusive claim to the street-cleaning jobs dispensed by the Vare organization. However, connections with the Italian bosses were established within this system itself. The workers had to belong to the Mutual Aid Society (Società Operaia di Mutuo Soccorso) as a condition of employment, and the society was controlled by the immigrant bosses.*[25]

Dues for Mutuo Soccorso di San Biagio were paid according to age. To join, members had to pay $2 (between eighteen and twenty-five years old), $3 (between twenty-six and thirty-five), $4 (between thirty-six and forty) or $5 (between forty-one and forty-five). Each member paid $1.50 every three months and a funeral tax of $0.25. The society's purpose was to help the families of members. If a member died, his wife would receive $100. The group met every other Sunday.

Mutuo Soccorso di San Biagio in front of Baldi Real Estate building. *Victor Baldi Collection.*

Among the bosses and *padroni* in Philadelphia, one stood out above the others:

> *Philadelphia's pre-eminent* padrone *was C.C.A. Baldi. But Baldi was neither a typical immigrant nor a mere gang boss. Indeed, by 1900 Baldi had become the respected leader of the Italian community, honored by Italian royalty and American officials. Although his beginnings were humble, Baldi rose quickly, in part due to his* padrone *activities. During the 1890s he was called upon to arbitrate a strike of the Schuylkill Valley Railroad system, a reflection of his growing reputation as a mediator between the industrial matrix and the immigrants.*[26]

CHAPTER 5

THE COAL YARD

FIRST LARGE BALDI BROTHERS BUSINESS

The brothers got into the coal business in a very circuitous way. In 1883, C.C.A. was already an interpreter for the courts in Philadelphia. His English was obviously good enough to be so appointed. That year, Thomas F. Karanse, a contractor laying track and ballast for the Schuylkill Valley Railroad, asked C.C.A. to come up to Pottsville as an interpreter to work with the Italian laborers or *tracca ganga* because of a strike. Historian Richard Varbero recounted the event in a letter to C.C.A. Baldi's son Vito in July 1970:

> *During a strike involving Italian laborers against the Schuylkill Valley Railroad, Baldi was sent upstate by the Italian consel as an interpreter and advisor. Applying a deft touch, Baldi resolved the dispute and was rewarded with a paymaster's job by the railroad company. As one account has it, Baldi subsequently became a contractor's Superintendent in the Pennsylvania anthracite region. As "boss" of the "tracca ganga" or a variant of the classical* padrone*, the alert Baldi discovered that hard coal was being employed for fill. Shrewdly, he contracted to supply dirt for the coal, "wagon load for wagon load." He shipped the fuel back to Philadelphia to a coalyard at Twelfth Street and Washington Avenue. The coalyard was but one of the horizontally integrated businesses that Baldi organized.*

The Schuylkill Valley Railroad had a unique advantage: from the upstate anthracite coalfields to the city is a continual descent of eighty-three miles, thus enabling longer trains of coal cars to be hauled down to Philadelphia.

Frangini has a version from 1907 that is consistent with what I was always told by my father—namely, it was that C.C.A. found a rock quarry and got the railroad to agree that crushed rock was as good as or better to lay rails on than hard coal, and as long as he could swap out ton for ton, the railroad said take the coal. Sparks could set the coal on fire, but crushed stone had no such risk. Coal was the fuel most used to heat houses and run furnaces. The brothers, according to Frangini's book, opened the first store for coal among the Italians in Philadelphia.

The advantages of selling anthracite coal were twofold: it burns hotter than other coals or wood, and it burns longer. It also produces virtually no smoke or particulate emissions.

In 1914, a coal yard at 1232 and 1238 Washington Avenue and shops at Thirteenth and Washington were sold by John Russell to Joseph F.M. Baldi for a "nominal consideration" and assumption of a mortgage of $25,000.[27] Seven years earlier, it was brother Virgilio Antonio Baldi who historian Frangini said was the head of the coal business.

In 1917, during World War I, the Philadelphia district attorney opened a price-fixing probe of coal dealers to determine if they had agreed to raise the price of coal at the same time. Seven retail coal dealers denied the allegation. Among those questioned was Joseph F.M. Baldi, a member of the firm of C.C.A. Baldi and Brothers.

Eleven years later, in 1928, the company's president, C.C.A. Baldi, was fined fifty dollars for violating a city ordinance making it unlawful to deliver

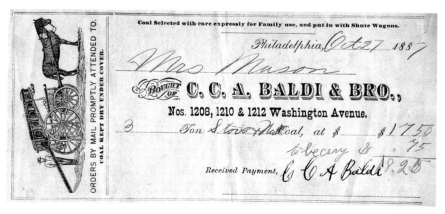

An 1887 coal receipt. *Robert Baldi Collection.*

Above: A cardboard ink blotter given out to customers. *Author's collection.*

Right: A cartoon of Joseph and Carmen Baldi in 1929. Philadelphia Inquirer, *from author's collection.*

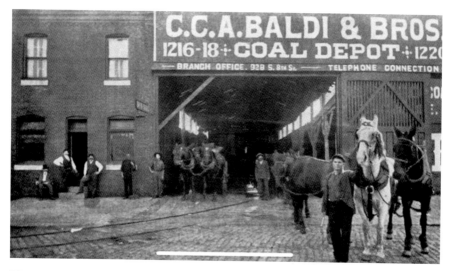

The coal yard. *Victor Baldi Collection.*

coal less than 2,240 pounds to the ton. The complaints were pursued by the Better Business Bureau. Joseph F.M. Baldi represented the company as its counsel and blamed "carelessness on the part of some employees."[28]

By 1929, C.C.A. Baldi, Jr., was running the coal company, and an *Inquirer* cartoon showed him and his brother Joseph F.M. Baldi as two representatives in the state legislature. Holding a bucket of coal is C.C.A., Jr., captioned "South Philadelphia," and Joseph as "Roxborough" for their two districts. The companies were in South Philadelphia, but C.C.A. Sr. lived in Roxborough at 319 Greene Lane, where his son Joseph also resided.

C.C.A. Sr. died in 1930, when the Depression was underway. The coal business went under at some point in the 1930s. In 1936, a short weight controversy dogged the company when the mayor ordered all city contracts for coal canceled after the company was accused of shorting the city by 603 tons.[29] The mayor also suspended the city's chief inspector responsible for oversight of coal purchases.

My father, born in 1915, said he understood the city bought Baldi coal that was piled up on piers. The front along the streets had a big pile of coal, but the rest of the pier had no coal behind it, and that was the scheme that led to trouble. C.C.A., Jr., denied any knowledge of short-weighting.

C.C.A. TAKES A WIFE

In 1886, C.C.A. married Louisa Eurindine Sobernheimer of Philadelphia. She was born in Philadelphia on May 16, 1860, and died in March 1924 at the age of sixty-four. The marriage license index for 1885–1916 maintained by the Orphans Count shows the license number as 2663 in 1886. In the same records under C.C.A. Baldi, the year is given as 1888 for license 2663, so it is obviously a typo.

Louisa's parents were immigrants from Rheinland Pfalz or Rhineland Palatinate in Germany. Their town was Bad Sobernheim. *Bad* means there was a bath or spa there from ancient times. Someone from Sobernheim is a Sobernheimer (as in "I am a Berliner"). That Germanic influence is reflected in C.C.A.'s appreciation of the unifier of Germany (as Garibaldi had unified Italy), one Otto von Bismarck, known as the Iron Chancellor (1815–1898). Thus, we have Virgil Bismark Baldi and his progeny.

The town of Bad Sobernheim had a population of 6,420 in 2013. Today, half are evangelicals and 25 percent are Catholic. In 1808, there were 64 Jews, which rose to a peak of 135 in 1895. The nearest large city is Kaiserslautern, which had 98,166 people in 2014.

A photograph of young Louisa (daughter of Fred and Katherine) taken in Kaiserslautern is included here. On the back of it are dates ranging from 1889 to 1900, so she must have returned to visit family still in Sobernheim.

Louisa's father was Frederick Sobernheimer, and her mother was Katherine Luisa Sobernheimer, born in Bavaria on November 19, 1836. She died on February 18, 1928, at age ninety-one, having outlived her daughter.

Clockwise from top left: Louisa Sobernheimer; C.C.A. Baldi; Louisa Sobernheimer as an older woman; Frederick Sobernheimer. *Author's collection.*

Clockwise from top left: Frederick Sobernheimer, Jr.; Emily Sobernheimer; Lottie Sobernheimer; Harry Sobernheimer. *Author's collection.*

Left to right: C.C.A., Jr., Louisa Sobernheimer, Rose, Louise, Joseph and Virgil Baldi on the steps of Green Lane. *Author's collection.*

Above: Louise Baldi
(Douglas) at Green Lane
with her mother, Louisa.
Author's collection.

Right: Louisa
Sobernheimer Baldi and
her grandson Charles
G. Douglas, Jr. *Author's
collection.*

The photos of their children Frederick, Jr., and his siblings are on page 32. Emily was also known as Emma. Neither Lottie nor Emily married.

Fred and his son, Frederick, Jr., were both lawyers practicing together in Philadelphia. They all lived at 319 Green Lane in Roxborough.

The family were Presbyterians, and C.C.A. and his children were too. C.C.A. was raised a Catholic in Italy, and after his wife died in 1924, he moved to an apartment in South Philadelphia over the bank and returned to his Catholic roots.

Louisa Baldi died in 1924 at home, at 319 Green Lane, of heart trouble.[30] The article on her death in the *Inquirer* said, "She has been active in charitable work, especially in connection with the First Presbyterian Church in Manayunk."[31] She was buried in Westminster Cemetery near Manayunk in Roxborough in the Baldi family crypt, built in 1920 by C.C.A. Louisa died a year after the bombing of her home by anarchists or socialists, as discussed in chapter 17. Douglas Swift's mother, Rose Baldi Douglas, one of C.C.A.'s granddaughters, related that Louisa's health had declined in the year following the bombing in 1923.

The lead author's grandmother Louise Baldi Douglas, daughter of C.C.A., sang and played the piano at numerous concerts. The annual concert at the New Century Drawing Room on March 28, 1910, was written about in the *Inquirer*,[32] as was one in April 1910.[33] Ten years later, Louisa Baldi, Rose Baldi and Emma Sobernheimer were part of the cast of entertainers at the Thursday Night Club at a home on East Hermitage Street.[34]

In 1913, tragedy struck the Sobernheimer family when young Frederick A. Sobernheimer, Jr., took his life at the Bellevue-Stratford Hotel. A letter to a woman and a new pistol with one round fired were found on his hotel bed, along with the fully clothed body of Frederick, Jr. He had graduated from the University of Pennsylvania in 1910 and was a graduate of Central High School.[35] C.C.A. accompanied Frederick, Sr., to the hotel and rose to the occasion by asserting that the gun "was accidentally" discharged.[36] The news article said the address of Frederick, Jr., was 323 Green Lane in Roxborough, and his law practice was with his father in the Stephen Girard Building.[37] Frederick, Jr., was an only son.

CHAPTER 7

THE BROTHERS INCORPORATE

A fter success selling coal, C.C.A. and brothers Virgil and Joseph started an undertaking business, a livery stable and had real estate interests. Virgil was in charge of coal, Joseph undertaking and livery and C.C.A. the real estate and later banking interests. The entity all these operated under was C.C.A. Baldi & Brothers.

An 1887 city directory shows the three brothers doing business at 4804 Washington Avenue. An 1888 directory listed under Coal Dealers one C.C.A. Baldi at 1208 Washington Avenue. An 1890 directory lists two Baldi undertaker addresses at 2018 Girard Avenue and 928 South Eighth Street.

Virgilio was born in Italy in 1864 and died in 1957 at age ninety-three without family, according to Victor Baldi, III. Brother Giuseppe (Joseph) Fioravanti Menotti Baldi was born on February 16, 1870, in Italy and came to Philadelphia in 1887.

In 1909, a property the Baldi brothers owned at 828 Christian Street had a saloon on it run by a Michael Vozzelli. Vozzelli had been financially backed by Joseph Baldi, who paid to have the annual liquor license renewed without Vozzelli's consent. According to a court filing by the saloonkeeper, a dispute arose out of a $15,000 note that Joseph held and wanted Vozzelli to pay.[38]

In 1911, the king of Italy honored brother Joseph for his "active interest in the advancement of his fellow countrymen" by bestowing on him the title of chevalier (or cavalier) five years after doing so for C.C.A.[39] At the time, Joseph was living in Newark, New Jersey. In June 1911, a banquet in the new chevalier's honor was held in Philadelphia, attended by Mayor Reyburn and the Italian Consul, among other dignitaries.[40] In 1915, Joseph went home to Castelnuovo Cilento to be with his mother, Rosa, during a serious operation. While there, he fell ill with typhoid pneumonia.[41] He later returned to live in Italy and died there at age fifty-six in February 1927.[42]

Joseph Fiorovanti Menotti Baldi. *From Donna di Giacomo, Italians of Philadelphia (2007).*

For years, Joseph had been appointed as an inspector of the Philadelphia County Prisons. He was also a director of *L'Opinione* and a member of the Manufacturer's Club and the Young Republicans and a director of the Italian Federation.

The Bristol, Pennsylvania paper reported that a branch of the Joseph F.M. Baldi undertaking business was established there with Luigi Galzerano as its manager, with J.M. Galzerano having recently taken over the business. The Galzeranos were the family Joseph and C.C.A.'s father, Vito, had married into when he took Rosa Galzerano as his wife.

The 1893 city directory lists just one undertaking address at 928 South Eighth Street, coal at 1229 Washington Avenue and the home for C.C.A. at 319 Green Lane in Manayunk. Sometime near the end of the 1890s, younger brothers Guerino and Alfonso came to Philadelphia from Italy to join the business team.

In 1905, the brothers branched across the Delaware to Camden, New Jersey, according to the *Inquirer*:

Baldi Brothers Get a Charter

The Charles C.A. Baldi Brothers & Co. was incorporated in Camden, yesterday, with a capital of $300,000, the object being to deal in coal, lime, wood and to board and furnish laborers in all parts of the world. The incorporators are C.C.A. Baldi, J.M. Baldi, Virgillo [sic] A. Baldi, of Philadelphia, and E.S.C. Bleakley, Camden.

Ads from the Italian-language newspaper *L'Opinione* pitched C.C. Baldi Bros. & Co. as agents and brokers for real estate. It reads:

Now is The Time To Buy Property at a Low Price

If you want to buy or sell or you need a mortgage or you have property to rent before trusting blindly to unknown or inaccurate people, consult our well known company.

The four-story building in South Philadelphia has signs for C.C.A. Baldi Bros. & Co. for real estate; loans and mortgages; and fire, life and accident insurance. The brothers loaned money, bought properties and managed rental properties for themselves and others. Professor Luconi said C.C.A.'s activities in real estate "earned him the title of 'slumlord.'"[43] The 1914 value of his holdings—including funeral homes, stores, a hotel, a factory, a warehouse and more—came to $149,150, according to the professor.

An article in the *Inquirer* in 1909 described how C.C.A. bought properties at 1224–30 Washington Avenue consisting of two three-story buildings and two-story buildings on a lot measuring 80 by 130 feet. It was described as "an addition to his plant" at Twelfth Street and Washington Avenue.[44]

Being a landlord had its ups and downs. When a reporter asked C.C.A. Baldi about the address of a property he owned that might have had immoral

Left: Guerino Baldi. *Right*: Alfonso Baldi. *From Donna di Giacomo*, Italians of Philadelphia *(2007)*.

Baldi Brothers Real Estate ad in *L'Opinione*. *Victor Baldi Collection.*

activities being conducted on it, he said his company was agent or property manager for "many that we do not know the tenants."[45] When asked what he would do if he received official notice about prostitution at an address owned or managed by his company, C.C.A. said the house would be vacated "in less than fifteen minutes."[46]

An eviction case before a Philadelphia rent oversight committee showed C.C.A.'s interest in fighting domestic violence. The case was reported as follows:

Antonio Rapacili of 1232 Latonia Street, said that his landlord, C.C.A. Baldi had raised his rent from $22 to $30, and now insisted that he give up the house.

The sympathy of the committee quickly disappeared, however, when the witness said he had bought a house two doors distant, but could not move because the tenants in the house he had bought would not get out, as they had no place to go.

Mr. Baldi testified that the house had been sold to a man now living in a suburb who wishes to occupy the building. He said he had offered to rent three rooms to Rapacili until he could get into his house.

"Why didn't you take those rooms" Rapacili was asked.

"I was afraid I could not meet the terms."

"What were the terms," a member of the committee asked Baldi.

"I told him he could have the rooms if he would stop his children from yelling all the time and stop fighting with his wife, and he said he didn't know whether he could promise."

Rapacili nodded approval of the answer and was told that under the circumstances he would have to get out of the house.[47]

In 1925, a thirty-seven-house project in Media outside Philadelphia was reported under the control of Joseph Baldi:

Among the recent projects announced for construction in this city's suburbs was an operation of thirty-seven houses, which Joseph F.M. Baldi and others of this city, propose to erect in Media. The development is known as Schenley Estates and will include dwellings, two and one-half stories high, of brick, hollow tile and stucco construction.

Sale of ten lots in this development for erection of as many homes was reported a week ago.[48]

Insurance was another enterprise the brothers engaged in. Prudential Insurance Co. of North America was founded in 1875 in Newark, New Jersey, to sell burial insurance. It later evolved into life insurance products, and at least by 1928, a Prudential group life policy was sold to twenty-one employees of two barbershops in Newark. The news article, titled "Prudential Insures Barber Employees," said the two barbershops were the "first concern of this type to take out group insurance" in Newark. The officers of Clinton Building Barber Shop, Inc., included Charles A. Baldi as vice president.[49]

The four brothers running the family businesses appear here. Both C.C.A. and Joseph Fiorovanti were knighted by King Victor Emmanuel, III, as chevaliers in 1907 and 1911, respectively.

With sons of the brothers including a doctor and two lawyers, it is their combined callings that made up a fair share of the *prominenti* cited in research by the Italian government: "According to an inquiry into Italian businessmen and entrepreneurs that the local Italian consulate conducted throughout Pennsylvania, in 1909 Philadelphia numbered ten lawyers, sixteen physicians, thirty-one contractors as well as forty-one bankers and steamship agents."[50]

Clockwise from top left: C.C.A. Baldi; Joseph F.M. Baldi; Alfonso Baldi; Virgilio A. Baldi. *From Donna di Giacomo*, Italians of Philadelphia *(2007)*.

ITALIAN EXCHANGE BANK

FRANK ROMA BROTHERS & CO.

C. C. A. BALDI, President

AGENZIA GENERALE DELLA

: CUNARD LINE :

Si rilasciano biglietti di passaggio per tutte le
linee di navigazione

Si occupa di qualunque affare bancario

Vaglia postali e rimesse telegrafiche al miglior cambio
della giornata

Tratte e Lettere di Credito sopra le principali citta'

CARTA ITALIANA E ORO

Compra e vendita di Rendita Italiana. Depositi.
Ufficio notarile

SERVIZIO DELL' UNITED STATES EXPRESS CO.

925-927 SOUTH NINTH STREET

PHILADELPHIA, PA.

C. C. A. BALDI		F. ROMA
V. A. BALDI	BOTH TELEPHONES	L. ROMA
F. G. M. BALDI		E. ROMA

Top: Italian Exchange Bank newspaper ad for the Cunard Line. *From Michael di Pilla*, South Philadelphia's Little Italy *(2016).*

Bottom: Baldi Brothers building. *Victor Baldi Collection.*

With all of the coming and going to Italy, it was quite natural for ticketing and financing steam travel to go together as businesses. The Italian Exchange Bank was founded in 1903, when three Roma brothers joined three Baldis, who had the exclusive right to ticketing in Philadelphia for the Cunard Line. Immigrants could open a passbook savings account to save up for passage or borrow to bring a relative over.

On September 13, 1914, the *Inquirer* reported that Virgilio A. Baldi had recently returned from Naples.[51] In 1923, the *Public Ledger* reported that C.C.A. Baldi had sailed from Italy to return home after a "pleasure trip."[52]

In 1910, a book titled *Americans of Italian Descent* contained a picture of the Baldi brothers building (seen on page 42). Under the photograph was a description in Italian of the Fratelli (Brothers) Baldi, with a glowing account of their businesses. The translation is:

> *We have in the Baldi brothers—An example of what can be done by the activity and work of an Italian in America. They ascended from the selling of fruit, to today directing an industrial multiplex of the first order. The sale of wholesale coal, a real estate office and a banking institution, all united and administered admirably. They instituted a cigar factory, a work center for the Italians, a fountain of pure water in the neighborhood, and the cleaning up of the area (where the establishments are), previously overwhelmed by the odors of a tannery. In addition, they donated a three-story building to be used as a hospital for Italians. They sought initiatives of the church, school, monuments and local charitable associations, defending Italians in prison and deceased. The magnitude of the patriotic deeds are documented and characteristics of the Baldi brothers have merited praise, both locally and nationally.*
>
> *Recent Cavalier C.C.A. Baldi presented before the Commissioner of Immigration in Washington a passionate defense of many Italian immigrants. Many times he has been chosen to represent the City of Philadelphia, and ultimately it was Mayor Reyburn who delegated him to be one of the ten representatives for Philadelphia in the 3rd Annual Convention of the Atlantic Deeper Waterway Association held in Providence, Rhode Island last September 30.*
>
> *Here is how an Italian can be proud of himself, of his colony and his Fatherland.*

Brother Guerino Carmelo (William) Baldi was born on January 2, 1875. In 1905, he married Bessie L. Cowperthwaite in Philadelphia. He died on June 25, 1909, and the *Inquirer* listed his name in the death notice as Guerino William Baldi.[53] Brother Alfonso is discussed in the following chapter.

CHAPTER 8

THE BALDI FUNERAL HOME

The only Baldi Brothers legacy business still ongoing is run by Victor L. Baldi, III, of South Philadelphia, the great-grandson of C.C.A. Baldi's brother Alfonso Baldi. The Baldi Funeral Home at 1331 South Broad Street in South Philadelphia was established a century ago in 1921.

The brothers became involved in the undertaking business in the 1880s because Italians were superstitious of non-Italian facilities. There is also a story of Italians being treated poorly that motivated C.C.A. to start a business for which he had no prior experience:

> *While collecting bills one day, Baldi met an undertaker, who spoke slightingly of the Italians and boasted of the fact that he had a corner on the burial business.*
>
> *Baldi reminded the man that it was bad business policy to speak so ill of his fellow countrymen, and finally told him there would be another undertaker in the Italian colony within 60 days. In less than that time a sign was displayed, "C.C.A. Baldi & Bros., Undertakers," in a shop on 5th street below Christian.*
>
> *The same spirit which dominated the boy who sold lemons was more empathetic in Baldi the undertaker. Things reached such a stage it is said that the establishment had eight or nine funerals in a single day.*[54]

Son Vito also became an undertaker at Thirteenth and Federal Streets in South Philadelphia. An ad for his place said it was sanitary, "professionale,"

Servizio inappuntabile in qualunque punto della Città
Aperto giorno e notte.

Telefono: HOWard 4042

VITO M. BALDI
Imbalsamatore ed Impresario di
Pompe Funebri
RESIDENZA

S. E. Cor. 13th & Federal Streets
PHILADELPHIA, PA.

Un funerale moderno può essere elaborato o semplice, secondo i desideri o le condizioni della famiglia interessata.
Le tradizioni della civiltà hanno stabilito ben definite regole per la condotta di ogni servizio funerario.
La prima e più importante regola è la preservazione della salma. In questo, come in ogni altro ramo del genere, la VITO M. BALDI SERVICE rende sempre il miglior servizio possibile. Servizio "professionale", sanitario, dignitoso, racchiudente in sè, nel medesimo tempo, tutte le qualità della cortesia, dell'economia, della discrezione e della efficienza amministrativa. Nel VITO M. BALDI SERVICE, non vi sono preoccupazioni nè ansietà di sorta.
Ogni dettaglio di un funerale è trattato con la più scrupolosa precisione e delicatezza, col solo intento di soddisfare la dignità e i sentimenti di affetto della famiglia colpita dal dolore.

Left: Ad for Vito M. Baldi Funeral Home in 1932. *From Donna di Giacomo,* Italians of Philadelphia *(2007).*

Below: Funeral cards for both funeral homes, 1940–41. *Victor Baldi Collection.*

"Blessed are they that mourn, for they shall be comforted."
St. Matt. v. 4

My Jesus have mercy on the soul of

Maria C. Ciapparone
Died December 11th, 1941

PRAYER

O Gentlest Heart of Jesus, ever present in the Blessed Sacrament, ever consumed with burning love for the poor captive souls in Purgatory, have mercy on the soul of Thy servant MARIA bring her from the shadows of exile, to the bright home of Heaven, where we trust, Thou and Thy Blessed Mother have woven for her a crown of unfading bliss. — Amen. Eternal rest grant unto her. O Lord! and let perpetual light shine upon her! May her soul and the souls of all the faithful departed rest in peace. Amen.
Sacred Heart of Jesus, have mercy on her.
Immaculate Heart of Mary, pray for her.
St. Joseph, friend of the Sacred Heart, pray for her. — (100 days).

Vito M. Baldi, Funeral Director,
S. E. Cor. 13th & Federal Sts., Phila.

"We have loved her during life; let us not abandon her, until we have conducted her by our prayers into the house of the Lord." —St. Ambrose.

My Jesus have mercy on the soul of

ADELINE MILONE
DIED, JANUARY 15th 1940
PRAYER

O gentlest Heart of Jesus, ever present in the Blessed Sacrament, ever consumed with burning love for the poor captive souls in Purgatory, have mercy on the soul of Thy departed servant.

Be not severe in Thy judgement, but let some drops of Thy precious Blood fall upon the devouring flames and do Thou, O merciful Saviour, send Thy angels to conduct her to a place of refreshment, light and peace. Amen.

Eternal rest grant unto her, O Lord, and let perpetual light shine upon her. Sacred Heart of Jesus, have mercy on her, Immaculate Heart of Mary, pray for her. St. Joseph, friend of the Sacred Heart pray for her.

(100 days for each aspiration)

C. C. A. BALDI BROS. & CO., INC.
VIRGIL B. BALDI
Undertakers

1011 So. 8th St.   Phila., Pa.

modern but dignified. As late as 1941, an in memoriam card for Maria Ciapparone was from Vito M. Baldi, funeral director. Another funeral for Adeline Milone reflected it was conducted at C.C.A. Baldi Bros. & Co., Inc., Virgil B. Baldi Undertakers, at Eighth and Kimball Streets.

In 1905, C.C.A. Baldi put out to bid an architect's plans for a stable and undertaking establishment:

Plans have been finished by Architect J. Elvin Jackson and estimates have been invited by Wanner & Stinson for an undertaking establishment and stable for C.C.A. Baldi, on Montrose street, below Ninth. The drawings show a three-story and basement brick structure, 34.4½ x 90½ feet. A bowling alley, engine, boiler and dynamo rooms will be fitted up in the basement; a mortuary, dead room, offices and a carriage room on the first floor; stalls for horses on the second floor, and a hay loft and carriage house on the third floor. Bids for the work are due on March 13.[55]

The 1907 book *Pennsylvania and Its Public Men* described the business:

The undertaking branch is said to be the largest in the city. It occupies a colossal building, 65 by 300, 1011 to 1017 S. Eighth Street. All the modern appliances are found in it. It was formerly occupied as the site of a tannery, the stench of which was offensive, and it was really to abate this nuisance that the Baldi Brothers bought the property and invested many thousands in the new structure. It has a large filter plant which furnishes coal and pure water free to the people, and which is a great blessing to the poor.[56]

Baldi Funeral Home around 1900.
Victor Baldi Collection.

Frangini's 1907 book also discussed the funeral home, but in Italian. A translation obtained by Victor Baldi, III, provides the following description:

It is a large building that occupies a surface of 65 to 360 feet, to 3 floors and a half, to 6 for the other. In the foreground the office is furnished comfortably and elegantly and more than an artistic chapel for the funeral service, furnished with great luxury. It is decorated with stained glass, illuminated with trophies of electric globes.

On one side of the courtyard are dozens and dozens of luxury cars of every style and every elegance, always ready to get out of the garage.

In the second there is the stud farm with about 70 horses maintained with the most stringent hygiene systems.

In the same floor and other superiors there is attached a cigar factory, where they place hundreds of workers, most of them Italians. In the lower level, the basement, on the premises with walls and ceiling of wood, there is a "bowling" alley, reserved for the Baldi family; and then there is the beautiful machine, the latest model, which serves as steam heating in winter.

C.C.A. Baldi recalls that there was in that space, its early days of America, a sugar refinery, and fortunately for him he received a gift from the owners of the factory, of an empty barrel, which he puts as the center axis of bonfires in celebration evenings.

Between that empty barrel and the palace that all Americans today admire in Little Italy is contained a story of heroic sacrifices.[57]

It seems several brothers had their hands in the business. Frangini said that while C.C.A. Baldi "was superintendent of the overall company," Joseph (Fioravanti Giuseppe Menotti Baldi) ran the undertaking business and "became popular." The coaches and horsemen were not used just for funerals but also rented out for weddings, processions, baptisms and private trips or parties.

In 1909, thanks to C.C.A.'s active support of Republican causes, the Philadelphia coroner gave him rights to South Philadelphia for city undertaking work:

Councilman Rosenberg and Baldi Bros., Respectively, to Represent North and South Phila.

Coroner Ford announced yesterday the Appointment of Max Rosenberg and C.C.A. Baldi & Brothers as his official Undertakers: They succeed Oliver H. Bair, who held the position under former Coroner Jermon.

In dividing the work between two Undertakers Coroner Ford thinks that better service will be rendered. Undertaker Rosenberg has been assigned to the section north of Market street, while Baldi Brothers will look after what may be termed the southern section of the city.

Undertaker Rosenberg is Select Councilman and one of the Republican leaders of the Thirteenth ward.[58]

In 1913, C.C.A. was appointed by the governor to serve on the State Board of Undertakers. By 1925, a later governor, Gifford Pinchot, a Republican reformer, had removed C.C.A. from the undertakers' board after it had unanimously asked for his removal based on unspecified "abusive and intolerable" conduct.[59]

Baldi Loses State Position

Governor Pinchot in a letter today to Chas. A. Baldi, Philadelphia, announced his removal as a member of the State Board of Undertakers. The governor's letter said:

"I am in receipt of a formal communication from the other four members of the Board of Undertakers requesting your removal from the board on the grounds that your influence on the board is a destructive one and that you have retarded the progress of the board to a very great degree. Accordingly you are hereby removed from membership upon the State Board of Undertakers."[60]

Not one to back down from a fight, C.C.A. gave the press his response to the governor:

Ousted Undertaker Board Member
Gives Pinchot Hot Retort

Charles C.A. Baldi, dropped by Governor Pinchot this week as a member of the state board of undertakers because of what the governor called his "destructive influence," made public today his reply to the governor.

"If vigorous opposition to increase of expenditures in holding many unnecessary meetings of the board," wrote Baldi, "to listen to the academic discussion and presentation of the many fantastic and impractical theories

of several of the members rather than an orderly and reasonable dispatch of business, then I am out of tune with the board and humbly submit to the action you have taken."[61]

Half a year later, Chairman of the Board Edgar E. Eaton resigned, and his resignation was "promptly accepted" by Governor Pinchot. A news article said there had been differences on the board "over administration matters." It also referred to the earlier removal of C.C.A. "following a series of rows."[62] What was really behind all of this remains unknown.

Ties forged a century ago between the Baldi and Jacovini families continue today. In 1906, Grace or Grazia Baldi (1882–1963), the only sister among the brothers, was married to Peter or Pietro Jacovini (1883–1936) of Philadelphia. Pietro was head of the circulation department at C.C.A. Baldi's newly begun Italian-language newspaper, *L'Opinione*. The paper was next door to the funeral home at 1011 South Eighth Street. According to Victor Baldi, III, it was an arranged marriage.

In 1921, Pietro Jacovini established the Italian Burial Casket Co., located at 924–26 South Ninth Street, on the corner of Hall Street. A pioneer in the funeral business, he was one of the innovators of the prepaid funeral. Pietro sold funeral policies to families through an insurance company, collecting sometimes only pennies toward their funerals.

An accomplished inventor holding several patents, a civic leader and the editor of the only Italian daily newspaper of the time, *L'Opinione*, Pietro was seen annually leading the New Year's parade down Broad Street on his black stallion. After his passing in 1936, his three sons, William, Joseph and Pietro, Jr., were eager to expand the business to South Broad Street, a main avenue through the city. Together with their uncle Alfonso Baldi and his son Victor, Sr., a property (formerly a music conservatory) was purchased at 1327–29 South Broad Street. The name Pennsylvania Burial Co. Inc. was established in the new location, and with Baldi Funeral Home as a sister office, the two operated essentially as one business since 1943.

Over the years, three-story brownstones were purchased next to and across the street from the building and leveled to supply parking for services held at the establishment. These parking lots can hold in excess of one hundred vehicles for multiple services. The funeral home consists of four chapels, three on the first level and one on the second level with elevator access.

Above: Baldi Funeral Home in 2021. *Victor Baldi Collection.*

Left: *Top step, left to right*: Anthony LoBianco (secretary/treasurer), Peter Jacovini (funeral director/owner). *Bottom step, left to right*: Thomas Ngo (liaison to the Asian community/translator), Jennifer Close (office manager/director's assistant), Victor Baldi, III (funeral director/owner). *Victor Baldi Collection.*

BALDI
FUNERAL HOME
EST. 1921

Victor L. Baldi, III
FUNERAL DIRECTOR

Letterhead of the funeral home. *Victor Baldi Collection.*

Victor L. Baldi, III, is the current director of Baldi Funeral Home. He is shown on the previous page with his cousin Peter J. Jacovini—both fourth-generation funeral directors in Philadelphia.

The old neighborhood has changed over the years and now has a large population of Cambodian and Vietnamese people. As the funeral home website says:

> *In 1988 to better serve our Asian Community the second floor Chapel has been converted to accommodate the Buddhist Funeral Ceremonial. Cantonese, Mandarin Chinese, Vietnamese & Cambodian translation are available upon request. Because South Philadelphia has always been a melting pot for new immigrants Spanish translation is also available upon request.*

The Baldi family connections are reflected in the front-page story of January 14, 1931, in *L'Opinione* for the death of Antonio Laporta, their chief embalmer. The pallbearers were Virgil and Alfonso Baldi, as well as three of C.C.A.'s sons: Dr. Frederick S. Baldi, Joseph F.M. Baldi and C.C.A. Baldi, Jr. Laporta was born in Salerno and came to the "Stati Uniti," where he worked at C.C.A. Baldi Brothers.[63] His funeral was just two weeks after C.C.A.'s.

Alfonso Luigi Baldi was born in Italy on February 22, 1886, and came to the States at age seventeen in 1903. He married Theresa Simone. Alfonso and Theresa had three children: Victor Luigi Baldi, Alfonso L. Baldi and Frederick Virgil Baldi, all of whom are deceased. His funeral business was run with his son Victor, who was born in 1917 and died in 1952.

Above: A 1946 photo of (*left to right*) Frederick Baldi, Jr., Victor L. Baldi, Sr., Alfonso L. Baldi, Sr. (brother of C.C.A.) and Alfonso L. Baldi, Jr. *Victor Baldi Collection.*

Left: Alfonso Baldi, Sr., as a young man. *Victor Baldi Collection.*

Opposite, top: Victor L. Baldi, Jr., holding one son of Victor L. Baldi, III (*kneeling*), whose two sons are Louis and Victor. *Victor Baldi Collection.*

Opposite, bottom: Alfonso L. Baldi is in the middle row with his wife, Nina Gallo Baldi; the top row depicts Alfonso, III, Theresa, Anita and Ben; the bottom row is Patricia and Virginia. *Victor Baldi Collection.*

Victor, Sr., graduated from Upper Darby High School and the Dolan College of Embalming. He married Janice E. Cleres in 1940, and they had two children: Victor L. Baldi, Jr., and Candace E. (Baldi) Zulli. Victor, Sr.'s brother Fred became a doctor and Alfonso a chemical engineer.

CHAPTER 9

ITALIAN EXCHANGE BANK

T he Italians who came to America at first just wanted to earn money, save as much as they could and then go back to Italy. As Michael di Pilla observed in his book:

> Despite the fact that their wages were the lowest out of 23 immigrant groups, it is amazing how much was saved by Italian Immigrants. Italians earned about $1.50 to $2 a day at the beginning of the 20th century. However, they only needed 50 cents to live. They sent the rest home to their families in Italy to invest in land, to pay old debts, or to allow them some day to return to enjoy the fruits of their work. It was the opinion of the early Italians that German and Irish immigrants consumed everything they earned. The Americans wanted money earned in the country to be consumed here. It was believed by the editors of the newspaper L'Opinione that "for this reason there were restrictions against the Italians."[64]

The first Italian "bank" in 1885 was located at the corner of Catherine and South Eighth Streets. By 1893, there were twenty-five banks in Little Italy.[65]

> It is no wonder that there were so many banks in the neighborhood, as Italians invented banking. The word derives from banco, the name for the table where the early transactions took place in Florence and Venice. Ironically, the leaders of the bank in Florence were members of the Alberti

*family, who moved to Venice when the Medicis came to power. The Albertis
came to America in 1624, and their descendants are recorded as settling in
Philadelphia as early as 1759. Many Italian banks prospered and others
came on the scene until the stock market crash in 1929, when almost all
of these banks fell.[66]*

Most of the banks were not actually chartered as such but were an
amalgam of businesses with many facets.

*Essentially the bank was an agency for transmitting an alien's money
to his homeland. Transactions took place in the offices of a steamship
company, or at notary public or similar agencies. The immigrant bank
could do business out of a labor agency, saloon or pool hall, or even an
undertaking establishment. The immigrant bank, then, cannot be confused
with the institutions commonly identified as banking houses. In general, the
immigrant bank was a regular, uncharted institution which functioned as a
"general clearing house" for all economic affairs in the life of a foreigner.[67]*

The tie between steamships and "banking" was a natural one because
40 percent of the immigrants went back to Italy after earning money and
saving it here.[68] In fact, Americans referred to them as "Birds of Passage."[69]
It is against this background that a fully chartered bank was started in 1903
by the Baldi brothers. In 1903, the three brothers—Charles, Virgil and
Fioravanti—together with brothers Luigi, Franck and Emilio Roma formed
the Italian Exchange Bank–Frank Roma Brothers. Both families were from
the Salerno region, the Baldis from Castelnuovo Cilento and the Romas
from Calliano.[70] They had two offices on South Eighth Street, with the Baldi-
run building located at 928 South Eighth Street.[71] There was an apartment
above the bank that C.C.A. Baldi moved into after the death of his wife in
1924. He, in turn, died in that apartment in December 1930.

The Italian Exchange Bank was a family affair, with C.C.A. Baldi as
president, Virgilio as secretary and Joseph as treasurer. Vito M. Baldi, one
of C.C.A.'s sons, served as an officer as well as being a notary public, funeral
director and Republican ward politician.[72] In 1914, the three brothers and
C.C.A.'s sons Vito and Charles C.A. Baldi, Jr., applied to the governor for
a charter for the Italian Exchange Trust Company to sell title insurance.[73]

By 1923, the Roma name, which appeared in the Cunard Line
advertisement in chapter 7, was gone, as reflected in the letterhead of the
bank.

Left: The lobby of First Italian Exchange Bank. *From Frangini, Italiani in Filadelfia (1907).*

Below: 1923 bank letterhead. *Victor Baldi Collection.*

FIRST ITALIAN EXCHANGE BANK
C.C.A. BALDI & BROS.
PHILADELPHIA, PA.

CABLE
BALDIBROS

CORRESPONDENTI DEL
BANCO DI NAPOLI

March 1st, 1923.

Loyalty to customers is evident in four letters involving one John Lavina, who was in the Charlestown, Massachusetts prison in 1923. Lavina took with him to prison bank passbook number 25271 and supposedly asked to withdraw $1,000. Vito M. Baldi wrote back saying he needed to have that request confirmed by "another source" because the bank had earlier received different instructions from Lavina. The final letter from Vito indicates that he clearly smelled a rat, as he asked for a number of facts about the inmate and requested Lavina's signature and the original passbook among some of the items he needed. No response was forthcoming. (See the appendix for more information.)

Not all banks were as careful. In 1929, the Italian Merchants Bank was closed by the Commonwealth of Pennsylvania because of a cash shortage and a run on the bank. Pasquale Teti, a well-known banker, was jailed.[74] In 1929, there was a sharp downturn in the stock market that had ripple effects on banking by the fall of 1930. In 1930, there were sixteen thousand banks that did not belong to the Federal Reserve System. The bank from which a check was drawn and the bank in which a deposit was made each counted the sum as part of a bank's reserve. This double counting meant that the real cash reserved in banks was less than what the books recorded. Also, banks did not have cash in vaults sufficient to survive a run on the bank if scores of depositors in one day wanted greenbacks.

In November 1930, the Bank of Tennessee in Nashville closed its doors, and within weeks, hundreds of banks around the country had to suspend operations. Then on December 11, the fourth-largest bank in New York City ceased operations. Confidence in banks was dropping, and on December 28, 1930, C.C.A. Baldi died, and with that news came word-of-mouth concern about the viability of his bank. By January 5, 1931, the bank was closed by order of the Philadelphia County Orphans Court, according to the family's attorney, John J. McDevitt:

> *"The death of the founder and owner makes it necessary under the laws of the State of Pennsylvania that the affairs of the bank be liquidated through the Orphans' Court by his executors, Dr. Frederic Baldi, C.C.A. Baldi, Jr., Joseph F.M. Baldi, 2nd, and Virgil B. Baldi," McDevitt said.*
>
> *"The executors will liquidate the business as speedily as possible and the assets are ample to pay every depositor dollar for dollar."*[75]

An article in a San Diego newspaper reported that the Baldi bank's assets were $1 million, while deposits were only $800,000.[76] But the rumor clearly had a negative effect because the Philadelphia Chamber of Commerce posted a $10,000 reward for information leading to the arrest and conviction of any person or persons "spreading false and malicious information against any financial institution in Philadelphia."[77] Nonetheless, the bank was closed and never reopened.

CHAPTER 10

THE NEWSPAPER *L'OPINIONE*

The fourth and final leg of the chair that Baldi power sat on was the daily Italian-language newspaper *L'Opinione*, which began publishing in 1906. The newspaper's goals were to overcome village and regional rivalry and to foster a conservative Republican message to help get out the vote for the party. For twenty-seven years, it succeeded in those goals.

Abraham Lincoln, who secretly owned a newspaper in Illinois, observed, "Our government rests in public opinion. Whoever can change public opinion, can change the government." C.C.A. epitomized that view.

The flood of Italians to Philadelphia, New York and other cities was heaviest from the southern regions of Abruzzi, Basilicata and Calabria, as well as Sicily and Puglia. Philadelphia was home to the second-largest Italian American population in the United States.[78] In fact, by 1930, there were 182,368 first- and second-generation Italians in Philadelphia.[79]

However, it was not a united community but one of multiple colonies with different dialects and traditions based on the village or parish people came from.[80] Each village had its own patron saint and feast day, so there was diversity in the Catholic religious rites.[81] Even paganism was involved in some towns' rituals. For instance, the town of Cucollo in Abruzzi held a feast day on May 1 in honor of San Domenico Abate, who as a monk in the tenth century cleared a field of its snakes. Snakes are placed on his statue today as it is paraded through town as part of the Festa dei Serpani.

In 1852, Bishop John Neumann purchased land in Philadelphia at Seventh and Montrose Streets to construct St. Mary Magdalen de Pazzi Church to cater to Italians.[82]

Interior of St. Mary Magdalen de Pazzi Church (1852). *Temple University Library and Sons of Italy Lodge 2787.*

By 1910, Philadelphia had eighty-three Italian American societies "named primarily after the patron saint of a native village after some regional, provincial or local connection."[83] The Italian-language press mirrored that provincialism; the first newspapers targeted a region or province. For instance, an 1882 publication called *Il Vesuvio* clearly targeted readers from the Bay of Naples.[84] News from back home was always important because many Italians planned to save money and return to Italy.[85]

The immigrant press did help in political acculturation in America because life as a *paesan* in Italy had provided little in the way of active political involvement. "Aside from local matters, the immigrant press examined the international issues of socialism, anarchism, clericalism, and labor movement. Especially important were the rise of Fascism and the charismatic Benito Mussolini; both developments offered a political focus for Italian readers."[86]

In addition to births, deaths and marriages, the immigrant press helped to interpret the dynamics of American life, its laws and institutions.[87]

Professor Luconi has explained that to the Philadelphia Anglos and Irish, all of the "short and dark-skinned Italian Americans who often spoke only a little broken English" were all the same.[88] To them, a Wop "was a Wop, whatever his place of origin in Italy."[89] The Irish dominated the police force, so no matter your village, the "Irish policemen had harassed all Italians alike."[90] Anti-Italian sentiment and bigotry were strong. Outside of South Philadelphia, the Italians had to sit in a separate part of movie theaters.[91] Some places of employment had "Italians need not apply" signs. The Church of St. Paul had an Irish priest who denied baptism to an Italian baby girl in the early 1900s, "telling the parents to go to an Italian church."[92]

Ethnic antagonism between Italians and the Irish and Jews was attributed to the fact that the latter two groups were higher in the ethnic food chain as bosses and employers of Italian labor. Construction jobs were run by the Irish, while Italian tailors made up the bulk of the workforce for Jewish clothiers.[93]

Ironically, that prejudice gave an opening for *L'Opinione* to defend all things Italian and ignore the locality-based focus of prior newspapers. The Italian community became more Italian and less regional, which also advanced C.C.A.'s political grip on Little Italy.

L'Opinione maintained, "It is necessary we strike back effectively at a long tradition according to which Italian Americans can be denied everything just because they are of an ancestry of their own." That newspaper also urged Italian Americans to follow the example of the city's Germans and Irish, who reacted against the ethnic discrimination that had prevented their election to the public offices in Philadelphia by establishing two cohesive political organizations that allegedly swept away subnational divisions.[94]

The *prominenti*, like the Baldis, encouraged the Italians to think of themselves not regionally but as Italians first and not *paesani*.[95] The goal was to overcome parochial loyalties and identify as a group to take on the big city.[96] Ironically, "in a way it can be said that they became American before they were even Italian."[97]

After C.C.A. Baldi began *L'Opinione* in 1906, it became the main Italian-language daily and was the only daily after 1916, until it ceased publishing in 1935.[98]

A typical day in the editing department involved all the editors meeting in the early morning. Then they went out to the station house, city hall and other places to get the news. The director did not arrive until 11:00 a.m. He read the mail that the editing secretary had ready for him. At noon, the entire team went out to lunch. In the afternoon, the newspaper life intensified. At 3:00 a.m., dispatchers joined in. They provided their information to the linotypes, and the linotypes issued the type, which could then be corrected.

There were competing papers, and the main competitor was the evolving one published by brothers Arpino Giuseppe Di Silvestro and Giovanni (John)

Photo of the editors of *L'Opinione*. Editor Pietro Jacovini is seated in the center. He married C.C.A. Baldi's daughter Grazia. *From Michael di Pilla,* South Philadelphia's Little Italy *(2016).*

Di Silvestro. *Popolo* began as a weekly in 1899 and was consolidated with another paper to become *La Voce del Popolo*, the "voice of the people," as a daily in 1906.[99] By 1916, the Di Silvestros had discontinued that newspaper for a new weekly, *La Libera Parola*, a fighting liberal newspaper,[100] which became the voice of the Order of the Sons of Italy.[101]

A. Giuseppe Di Silvestro introduced the Sons of Italy to Philadelphia.[102] C.C.A. Baldi was also active in Italian fraternal associations and was president of the Circolo Italiano, which was "open to any Philadelphia professional of Italian descent."[103] A. Giuseppe Di Silvestro "acknowledged that he had conceived *La Voce del Popolo* as his mouthpiece to curb Baldi's growing influence in the Italian colonies due to *L'Opinione*.[104]

Two other weeklies came out in 1917 "as weapons in the conflict that pitted Baldi against the Di Silvestro brothers."[105] *La Rassegna* sided with Baldi and *La Ragione* with the Di Silvestros.[106] The rivalry also had to do with who would be "King of Little Italy" and enhance their role in dealing with the city's establishment, as well as representing the Italian community in national debates over issues like restricting immigration from Italy.[107]

In 1906, the year *L'Opinione* began, Congress started debating the merits of a literacy test to restrict immigration by excluding those who could not read or write in their native language.[108] It would have slowed the Italian migration dramatically, because at the turn of the twentieth century, 64 percent of arriving Italians were illiterate.[109] *L'Opinione* maintained that the literacy test was a "menace to Italians" as a whole, regardless of their native regions. A delegation to Washington, D.C., from South Philadelphia included major Italian associations headed up by C.C.A. Baldi.[110] They met with the Speaker of the House and President Theodore Roosevelt, both Republicans, as, of course, was C.C.A. The literacy test was not enacted until eleven years later under a Democratic president.[111]

As for issues related to labor disputes with management, *L'Opinione* was pro-management, consistent with its conservative bent. The paper would even run ads for strikebreakers when unions conducted work stoppages.

As with any strong persona, not everyone was enamored of C.C.A. Professor Varbero describes the press handling of Baldi's son Vito M. Baldi in a vote-stealing charge:

> *When Vito M. Baldi, for example, the politically active son of the Republican leader, was indicted in 1918 for the not uncommon Philadelphia practice of vote-stealing, the Italian press gleefully excoriated the younger Baldi.* La Libera Parola *described Vito Baldi as "the arch, the master conspirator," a manipulator of his fellow countrymen. Other weeklies sustained themselves briefly on political animosities; even the successful* La Libera Parola *held part of its audience by condemning local political figures as well as the Baldis.*[112]

The rivalries were fought out in the press, as there was no TV or internet to convey one's political positions:

> *As Baldi secured his grasp both as leader of the colony and as an ally of the Republicans,* L'Opinione *served as his political sounding board. A variety of Italian-Language periodicals vied with Baldi's daily, but none*

achieved the potency of circulation of L'Opinione. *Baldi, in fact, openly sneered at his journalistic rivals, likening La Forbice, for example to "a loser in a card game." He demeaned other papers as the products of nonentities who needed him, Baldi, for survival.*[113]

The Di Silvestro–dominated Circolo Italiano association attacked C.C.A. Baldi for "betraying" the Italians in Philadelphia, and some members signed a letter asking C.C.A. and his brothers to resign from the group.[114]

Among those who signed one letter denouncing Baldi as "an enemy of the Italians of Philadelphia" were Robert Lombardi, a fast-rising contractor; Eugene V. Alessandroni, a prominent young lawyer soon to be named Assistant District Attorney; Cav. Francis A. Travascio, an Italian undertaker highly prominent and active in professional circles; Rev. Tomasso della Cioppa; and Antonia Vegliona, an activist in fraternal orders.[115]

In 1918, the

alleged slight to the Italian community revolved about the elder Baldi's narrow selection of "respectables" for presentation to Mayor Thomas B. Smith; Baldi had excluded his political opponents from the list. Since an invitation, in this case to an honor banquet for the Italian missions, conveyed community prestige, the excluded Italians were incensed. The Baldi clan had struck "a mortal blow to the Italian colony," since they had selected only representatives from their own faction. Despite the comic aspects of such episodes, many Italians took such matters seriously, as evidenced by the protests of societies like the flourishing Societa Unione Abruzze and the Societa Barbieri, which angrily joined the repudiation of the Baldi faction.[116]

While the Italian press had begun to fade in importance by the 1920s, one fact still stood out: "The major political force within the community was headed by C.C.A. Baldi; his control of patronage jobs, allotted to him by the Republican machine, his daily means of communication, *L'Opinione*, and his leadership abilities made him immune to all but the most rhetorical flourishes of his ideological opponents."[117]

The end of *L'Opinione* began with the start of the Great Depression in 1929. Prior to the stock market crash, the weekly Di Silvestro paper, *La Libera Parola*, sold 32,190 copies a week, while the daily *L'Opinione* had a circulation

Front page of *L'Opinione*, June 29, 1914. *Victor Baldi Collection.*

of 35,107 copies.[118] The Depression caused a drop in advertising revenue. In December 1930, C.C.A. Baldi died, and his son Charles C.A. Baldi, Jr., inherited *L'Opinione*.[119] In 1933, the paper's shrinking profits forced him to sell it to Generoso Pope, a New York businessman who controlled a chain of Italian American newspapers.[120] Pope consolidated *L'Opinione* with his New York City–based *Il Progresso Italo-Americano* in 1935, but the result was only one additional page of Philadelphia news.[121] Pope later started the *National Enquirer*, the famous supermarket tabloid we still see today.

Copies of *L'Opinione* are not readily available, but there are microfilm copies in several libraries. The June 29, 1914, edition (seen on the previous page) led with the atrocity of the assassination of Archduke Ferdinand of Austria and his wife, Sophie, in Sarajevo that triggered the beginning of World War I.

CHAPTER II

IMMIGRATION AND LABOR

Professor Caroline Golab's book *Immigrant Destinations* relates that the Pennsylvania Railroad was "most responsible for initiating the Italian influx to Philadelphia."[122] The Philadelphia and Reading Railroad had miles of track and acres of railroads, so it employed large numbers of Italians as well.[123] Employers preferred them, but the workers did not stay long[124] and preferred "better paying jobs in the construction trades."[125] That, in turn, caused the *padroni* to recruit more workers from Italy to backfill the railroad jobs.[126]

> *Philadelphia's Italians were employed primarily as general laborers in unskilled occupations: construction work, especially street grading; sewer and subway construction; building and housing construction; street cleaning; street railway maintenance; snow shoveling; and scavenging (garbage and trash collection). Italian labor built City Hall, the Reading Terminal, and the Broad Street and Market Street subways.*[127]

C.C.A. Baldi and other Italian political leaders would organize newcomers into political clubs and associations in exchange for jobs tied to city contracts. The Italian workforce dominated street cleaning.[128] Another agreement gave them a monopoly "on street grading and the construction and maintenance of the city's railway lines."[129] Not all were in construction or railways. In 1900, barbers were 18 percent Italian and masons 8 percent.[130]

The labor force was not docile; by the end of 1907, over twenty thousand laborers employed by contractors in Philadelphia said they planned a strike after January 1, 1908. Their rate of pay was between $1.20 and $1.30 a day for a ten-hour workday. Their goal was $1.75 for eight hours of work. The *Philadelphia Inquirer* said the men "look upon C.C.A. Baldi and his brother Joseph as advisers and to these two they took their troubles."[131] The brothers advised them to do nothing "rash or precipitate" and wished them well.

On the night of December 14, 1907, workers met in Beneficial Hall at 920 South Eighth Street to form a union. They were addressed by Joseph F.M. Baldi and others.[132] A meeting was scheduled for a few days later with expectation of attendance being "tremendous, as the dissatisfaction spreads through all the Italian colonies."[133]

A few years later, it was the street cleaners' turn. More than five hundred street cleaners met in October 1913 at Lyric Hall located at Sixth and Carpinter Streets to peacefully petition their contractors to raise wages:

The workmen who are cooperating with "The Citizen's Street Cleaners Foremen's Labor League," seek an increase from $1.35 to $1.50 for wheelbarrow men on asphalt streets, and from $1.50 to $1.75 for those employed on thoroughfares paved with Belgian blocks. Frank Aiello presided at the meeting and Chevalier C.C.A. Baldi made the principal address. The latter told the men that their cause was a just one and predicted that the contractors would grant the increase requested. He urged them to conduct their movement in an orderly manner.[134]

The Vare brothers Republican machine combined with the Baldi brothers had "given Italian Americans a virtual monopoly on street cleaning positions," numbering 1,600 in 1914.[135] The ebbs and flows of Italian laborers became pronounced in early 1908, with a newspaper headline "Aliens Rush Back to Native Lands, Thousands Are Returning to Europe Taking Millions of America's Cash."[136] Joseph Baldi was consulted about the exodus:

"Scarcity of labor is driving the greatest number from our country," said Joseph F. Baldi. "I think the Italians and others are simply seizing an opportunity for seeing their families, many of whom are left in the old country to await a run of prosperity to bring them across to their husbands.

"It is my opinion that families are not leaving for the Italian settlement seems to be keeping quite well intact, and no very large number could leave without notice, especially among the Italians themselves."[137]

Eleven years later, after the end of World War I, the troops came home, and thousands of Italians headed in the other direction. An article in the *Inquirer* in 1919 reported that since the end of the war, "more than one hundred thousand Italians have left the United States."[138] C.C.A. Baldi was quoted at length and said high rent costs were part of the reason for the exodus. His concern was that once they got back to Italy, they might not be able to get back into the United States because most were not naturalized citizens and there were new immigration restrictions in effect.

> *"Industrial leaders should interest themselves more in these people and try to keep them here," said C.C.A. Baldi, Sr., yesterday. "The Italians are going back to Italy in large numbers at the present time. It is due to the unrest that they are experiencing in this country. They think the cost of living is too high and they are dissatisfied with the way things are going.*
>
> *"So they start drifting back to their own country, where they think conditions will be much better and they think the cost of living will be cheaper."*[139]

The second-highest employment category for Italians was in the clothing and tailoring business. In 1910, one-half of all women in the men's clothing industry of Philadelphia were Italian.[140] As for men in that industry, Italians were second only to Jews.[141]

> *Italian women like their Jewish counterparts, were often hucksters and peddlers; they were also operatives in the silk, cigar, artificial flower, and candy factories. Their greatest concentration, however, was as seamstresses, tailoresses, and finishers in their various needle trades. Indeed, the garment industry played a major role in keeping the Italians in Philadelphia: while husbands were paving streets, building sewers or unloading ships, wives could supplement family income by taking needle work into the home.*[142]

Immigration laws were a major issue due to the flood of immigrants coming to the United States from Italy, Ireland, Germany and more. A 1909 proposed tax increase on immigrants from four to ten dollars led to a coming together of all the ethnic communities under the banner of the United Societies of Philadelphia for the Relief and Protection of Immigrants. Members of Congress and the president were forwarded resolutions calling the tax increase unjust and ineffective.[143] The signers included the Friendly Sons of St. Patrick, the Association for Protection of Jewish Immigrants, the German Society of Philadelphia and the Italian Federation represented by its president, C.C.A. Baldi.[144] A year later, when over one hundred Italians were ordered deported by Commissioner Keefe of the federal Bureau of Immigration, the Jewish and Italian communities teamed up to fight Keefe's order:

Hebrews and Italians Demand Investigation of the Wholesale Deportation

C.C.A. Baldi and Attorney Go to Washington to Complain of Action of Commissioner Keefe

Aroused by what they term the harsh and unjust treatment of their country-men, a number of wealthy Italians and Hebrews of this city, headed by Charles C.A. Baldi, one of the wealthiest Italians in Philadelphia, and David Phillips, an attorney, yesterday went to Washington to demand an investigation by the Bureau of Immigration of the action of Commissioner General Keefe in ordering the deportation of more than a hundred steerage passengers on the Italian Line steamer Verona *and a score more from the American Line steamship* Merion. *The complaints assert that Commissioner Keefe, when he was in the city last week, misinterpreted the United States statute covering "assisted passage," and ordered the deportation of immigrants whose passage money had been sent them by relatives and friends residing in this country.*[145]

In an effort to stamp out the *padrone* system of contract labor, the law had changed to prohibit the admission into America of immigrants' ship passage paid by societies or corporations. They were termed in the law as "assisted immigrants." Hundreds were detained or refused admission on the *Verona* and the *Merion* by immigration authorities. Relatives and friends who came to unsuccessfully greet them "went at once to C.C.A. Baldi and other influential businessmen of South Philadelphia and complained."[146] The paper reported that "the residents of the Italian colony are thoroughly aroused."[147] The matter was to go before the head of the Department of Immigration in Washington, and "Baldi and his companions declare that they will spare neither effort nor money in having the case fully investigated."[148] After a visit to Washington, the commissioner general for immigration said that a relative's financial assistance was not illegal.[149]

A week later, Commissioner Keefe backtracked and released a majority of the detainees.[150] Ever one to put his money where his mouth was, six more were freed after C.C.A. Baldi paid a lawyer to obtain a writ of habeas corpus from a federal judge in the city.[151] One fifteen-year-old was saved by a court order just minutes before the ship *Ancona* was to return to Italy with him being deported.[152] Tragically, on the sail to New York to pick up more passengers, Antonio de Luca jumped into the Delaware and drowned. He was being sent back to Italy by the American authorities and was said to be "temporarily deranged as a result of being refused admission to this country."[153]

The *Ancona* and the *Verona* were built in 1908 in Belfast, Ireland, for the Italian Lines. They were designed as immigrant ships to go from Genoa and Naples to New York and Philadelphia. The *Ancona* was 8,200 tons and 482 feet long, with room for 2,500 steerage passengers and only 60 staterooms. During World War I, on November 8, 1915, a German U-boat sank the ship, and at least 300 people perished.

In 1913, a literacy test for immigrants finally passed Congress. Known as the Jones-Dillingham Immigration Bill, it aimed at getting a "better class of aliens" coming to our shores.[154] But the Philadelphia ethnic communities sent a delegation to meet with President Taft to urge a veto. The German-American Alliance, Association for the Protection of Jewish Immigrants, Polish-American Citizens League and the Italian Federation (represented by C.C.A. Baldi) made their case at the White House.[155] A week later, President Taft vetoed the literacy test bill, and it didn't become law until 1917, under President Woodrow Wilson. The message that C.C.A. Baldi and others made hit a responsive chord with Taft, who said in his handwritten veto message:

> *No doubt the law would exclude a considerable portion of immigration from southern Italy, among the Poles, the Mexicans and the Greeks.... The people who come from the countries named frequently are illiterate because opportunities have been denied them. The oppression with which these people have to contend in modern times is not religious, but it consists of a denial of the opportunity to acquire reading and writing. Frequently the attempt to learn to read and write the language of the particular people is discouraged by the government and those immigrants in coming to our shoes are really striving to free themselves from the conditions under which they have been compelled to live.*

The next major change affecting the Italians was in 1924, when Congress was considering a quota bill that would cut the numbers from southern Europe allowed into the United States. Once again, a delegation from Philadelphia went to fight an immigration bill. The Philadelphia Committee Against Racial Discrimination represented a 220-person organization in Philadelphia "comprising 200,000 naturalized and American born citizens."[156] The delegation met with Pennsylvania's senators and representatives to present their views. The delegation chairman was Dr. Leopold Vaccaro, and other members included assistant district attorney Eugene Alessandroni, C.C.A. Baldi and others:

> *Referring to the arguments used against southern immigrants that they do not become American citizens as quickly as the northern immigrants from Europe, the delegation stated that the northern immigration is an older one and may have a larger number of naturalized citizens. The Italians, however, it was asserted become naturalized within a short time after arrival, showing their willingness to become American citizens: that the delegates declared, should be taken as a criterion in establishing the quotas.*[157]

In the end, the Johnson-Reed Act passed, establishing a quota of 2 percent on each incoming nationality based on the 1890 census numbers. It cut Italian immigration from 42,057 to 5,802 per year.

CHAPTER 12

COLUMBUS, VERDI
AND ITALIAN PRIDE

I n the twenty-first century, there has been a push to cancel Columbus Day and replace it with some version of Indigenous People Day. In 2009, one hundred years after the Italian American community fought for a day to honor the prominent Italian sailor-explorer, Philadelphia canceled the annual Columbus Day parade that C.C.A. Baldi used to lead riding a white horse down Broad Street.[158] On July 4, 2020, a mob in Baltimore, Maryland, pulled down the Columbus statue and threw it into the harbor.

Columbus Day festivities began in Philadelphia in 1869.[159] For the fourth centennial in 1892, there was a coming together of the Philadelphia Italian community under an umbrella organization of the scores of associations to form the United Italian Societies of Philadelphia.[160] It included southerners like the Baldis, as well as prominent northerners like Emanuel V.H. Nardi. A book by local priest Father Isoleri was even published in Philadelphia for the 400th anniversary.

A year before, on March 14, 1891, a mob in New Orleans descended on a local jail and shot and mutilated eleven Italians. The police chief had been shot earlier, and before his death, a witness asked him who did it to him. He was claimed to have whispered back, "Dagoes." New Orleans was home to more Italian immigrants than any other southern city. When nine Italians were charged but not convicted of the late chief's murder, a massive mob went to the jail and conducted the largest mass lynching in American history. The effort to fight the racism against Italians evolved into the push for Columbus Day.

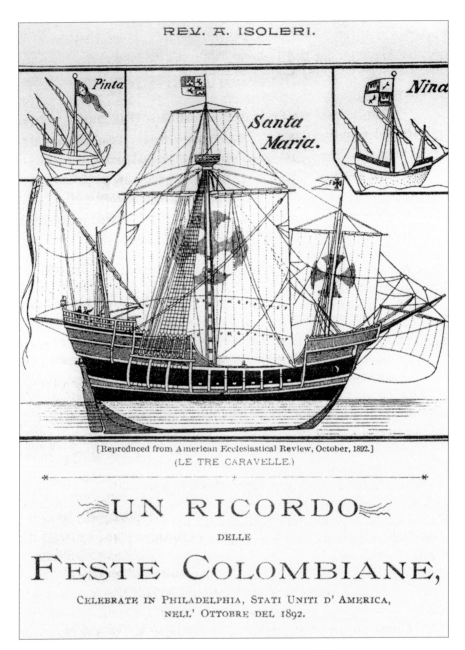

Above: Father Isoleri was born near Genoa and wrote a book in 1892 to commemorate the 400th anniversary of Christopher Columbus's voyage to the New World. *Courtesy of Celeste A. Morello. From Donna di Giacomo*, Italians of Philadelphia *(2007)*.

Opposite: "Italians Support Columbus Statue." *From* Philadelphia Inquirer, *1902*.

Ten years later, in 1902, C.C.A. Baldi, as head of the United Italian Societies of Philadelphia, was teaming up with Baltimore and New York Italians to erect a Columbus statue in Washington, D.C.

Mr. Baldi has been abroad now for nearly a month and has been making careful inquiry of some of the most noted sculptors with regard to the probable cost of the work proposed. He is expected to return towards the first of August, when he will be tendered a reception and banquet by prominent members of the many societies in the Italian colony of Philadelphia with which he is identified. At this gathering it is thought that the movement will take practical shape and that committees will be appointed to confer with representatives of kindred organizations of various other parts of the country.[161]

ITALIANS PLAN GRAND TRIBUTE

Proposed National Monument to Christopher Columbus at Washington

Ever since the monument to Count de Rochambeau at Washington was dedicated leading Italian residents of this city, New York and Baltimore have had in contemplation a similar movement looking to the erection of a grand statue of Christopher Columbus at the National Capital. The project has for the present been kept from general publicity pending a visit to Italy by Charles C.A. Baldi, who is at the head of the United Italian Societies of Philadelphia. The idea is to make the tribute to the memory of the discoverer of America a national one, in which all classes of people from the land where he was born may join.[162]

CHARLES C. A. BALDI

Ultimately, the group teamed up with the Knights of Columbus, and a grand statue was erected in Columbus Circle in front of Union Station in Washington, D.C., in 1912.

In 1909, there was a campaign to have Columbus Day made an official holiday in Pennsylvania:

Italians Want "Columbus Day"

Chevalier C.C.A. Baldi, representing the Italian colony of Philadelphia was here today and headed a delegation from several counties which called upon Governor Stuart and talked with many members of the Legislature in support of the proposition to have a legal holiday to be known as Columbus Day, in honor of the discoverer of America. There is a bill before the Legislature to provide for such a holiday.[163]

Columbus statue at Union Station in Washington, D.C. *Wikipedia.*

Italians in the northwest part of the city, including Manayunk and Germantown, organized for a celebration on October 12, 1910.[164] Teaming up again were Emmanuel and Samuel Nardi for the northern Italians and C.C.A. Baldi for the southern contingent at the event. The "orators" were a congressman and Professor Raphael de Luca, foreign editor of *L'Opinione*.[165]

In Baltimore, the United Societies of Baltimore took over Riverview Park for an all-day celebration with the Italian consul in attendance. "Commendatore C.C.A. Baldi, a Philadelphia banker, was the principal guest."[166] Commendatore was a title also given to C.C.A. by King Victor Emmanuel, III.

By 1915, working with the Knights of Columbus, the law had changed, making Columbus Day an official state holiday. At that year's celebration, Chevalier C.C.A. Baldi, president of the Italian Federation, announced that $5,000 raised for an Italian hospital (which was later built) was to be used instead for war relief. By that time, Italy was at war with Austria-Hungary.

In addition to Columbus, the Italian community also wanted to show pride in Italian composer Giuseppe Verdi. C.C.A. donated most of the funds for a Verdi monument in Fairmount Park. The seven-ton work was by the foremost sculptor of Italy, Ettore Ferrari of Rome.[167] The Italian Line ship

Ancona brought the work to Philadelphia at no cost. The eighteen-foot-high sculpture has a granite base and a bronze bust of Verdi.[168] It was unveiled on October 9, 1908, the anniversary of Verdi's birth. C.C.A. Baldi was the treasurer and chief fundraiser for the Verdi Monument Association.[169]

Said C.C.A.:

> *"This monument," said Mr. Baldi yesterday, "will not only be of sentimental interest as the gift of the great Italian public of the city to Philadelphia, but it will be a real object of art. Much of the statuary which is erected in this country in all cities here as well as in Philadelphia, is of a poor order of artistic merit. This is due to the absence of art juries and men of artistic feeling in legislative bodies as much as to lack of artists.*
>
> *"Philadelphia may rest assured that as a beginning for the art awakening that is sure to follow the completion of the Parkway and the art temples that will be built along it, this monument will stand as an example of the very best art of the twentieth century."* [170]

Verdi monument. *From Philadelphia Inquirer, October 10, 1908.*

At another ceremony in June 1917, the inventor of the wireless, Guglielmo Marconi; the mayor; Chevalier C.C.A. Baldi; and other dignitaries from Italy appeared in front of the Verdi monument.[171]

Natural disasters in Italy in the early 1900s led the *prominenti* like the Baldis, Nardis and Di Silvestros to advocate aiding fellow Italians as part of a common national peoplehood among the Italian newcomers and their offspring.[172] In 1905, there was an earthquake in Calabria, and in 1906, Campanians suffered from an eruption of Mount Vesuvius. The Di Silvestro brothers in their newspaper *Il Popolo* called for aid because "we are all brothers."[173] Unfortunately, there was a falling out when C.C.A. Baldi decided to exclude some of his detractors from a big fundraising dinner for victims of the Vesuvius eruption.[174]

When ethnic slurs against Italians occurred, it was always C.C.A. who spoke out. Thus, when the fifth officer of the *Titanic* said shots had to be fired to prevent Italian immigrants from jumping into the lifeboats for women and children, C.C.A., as president of the Italian Federation, made a trip to Washington, D.C., to question the officer.[175] He brought back an affidavit

Louise Baldi (Douglas), *second from left*, at the Verdi dedication. *Author's collection.*

from Fifth Officer Lowe that said he meant no slur but that there had been "some panic among the swarthy members of the Latin race."[176]

In 1915, when Italy entered World War I to get back territory in northern Italy it claimed should belong to it, Italian men in the armed forces living in the Philadelphia area who were reservists were ordered back to Italy.[177] This led to a destitute situation for their wives and children left behind in the city. C.C.A. Baldi, as treasurer of the official Italian War Relief Committee, raised thousands of dollars for the families.[178]

A year later, a fire left twenty-seven families homeless, so the Italian Federation, with C.C.A. as chairman, raised money for clothing and covered the first month's rent for new apartments.[179]

When Jewish groups sought to raise money for Jews suffering in World War I, they scheduled a fundraising concert. Among those sponsoring a box at the Metropolitan Opera House were Chevalier and Mrs. C.C.A. Baldi.[180] He was always willing to help others so that when he needed help, they would repay the favor.

Another issue of concern was the large numbers of immigrants from various countries for whom English was a second language. Pennsylvania was a huge melting pot of Irish, Germans, Jews, Italians and others. Those outside Philadelphia were then, as now, pushing English-only legislation. In

1919, Representative John Boland of Crawford County introduced a bill to repeal all laws that permitted official advertising to be printed in German, Yiddish or Italian, depending on the municipality.[181] A newspaper account of the bill said that "the Vare men of Philadelphia opposed the measure."[182] The intent was apparently due to "anti-German sentiment in the Legislature." The vote came just three months after the end of World War I and the battle against Germany's attempt to dominate Europe.[183] The vote to approve the bill in the Pennsylvania House was 143 to 28. The German, Italian and Jewish representatives from Philadelphia were among the 28 "no" votes, including C.C.A. Baldi, Jr.[184] Two weeks later, the House, by a vote of 180 to 7, prohibited the teaching of German in public schools.[185] Among the 7 "no" votes was that of C.C.A. Baldi, Jr.[186] In the 1950s, your author had three years of German in high school, but it was at Penn Charter, a private day school in Germantown.

By the end of 1919, the language battle had evolved into an option of offering Italian in schools. Since 1912, Italian had been an option for study in Philadelphia public schools, but it was dropped in 1919.[187] The city's associate school superintendent said it was dropped "because there was no demand for it."[188] Nonetheless:

> *Chevalier Baldi, as president of the Federation of Italian Societies, made his protest against the exclusion of Italian from a study course that makes French, Spanish, Greek, and Latin optional. "When you discriminate against the language of 500,000 soldiers killed, 1,000,000 mutilated," he said, "I must protest in the name of 200,000 people that you have offered an insult to all the Italian blood that was shed to gain the victory we are enjoying today."[189]*

When, in 1920, a United States senator from Tennessee referred to Italians as "Dagoes," the slur was met with outrage in Philadelphia.[190] The slur was uttered by Senator John K. Shields, who backpedaled by saying he meant no offense.[191] But fifteen thousand Italians, including hundreds of fathers and mothers of soldiers who fought for America in World War I, paraded down Broad Street to the Broadway Theatre in protest.[192]

The parade followed telegrams to the Pennsylvania delegation in Congress, including one from C.C.A. Baldi as president of the Italian Federation of Philadelphia, protesting the reference in the name of the thousands of Italian companions in arms of the American doughboys.[193] The parade was a massive outpouring of South Philadelphia pride:

The long parade, which was generously sprinkled with flags, all allied nations being represented as well as service flags, formed in companies at Eleventh and Christian streets and accompanied by several bands, one of which was an Italian military band, which saw service at the Italian-Austrian front, preceded by way of Christian street to Broad thence to the theatre.[194]

C.C.A. Baldi as keynote speaker at a Columbus Day event in Baltimore. *From the* Baltimore Sun, *August 16, 1921.*

Linking ethnic pride with being a good American, C.C.A., who presided, read the letter from Senator Shields and then, without commenting on Shields's statement, urged his audience not to give way to excitable impulses: "Remember you are loyal Americans, for to be true and faithful Americans means that you are at the same time truly representatives of Italians."[195] A year later, C.C.A. was the keynote speaker from Baltimore.[196]

The first Baltimore Columbus statue was erected in 1792 and the second in 1892 by the Italian United Society of Baltimore. The first influx of Italians to Baltimore were Genoese, and the explorer was born in Genoa.[197]

CHAPTER 13

EDUCATION AND AMERICANIZATION

With his formal schooling ending at age fourteen, C.C.A. Baldi was left with an enduring love for education that was manifested during and after his life. In a 1915 biographical article about C.C.A., it was reported that he went to night school and business school when he was selling lemons as a teenager but that most of his knowledge was acquired "in the school of experience."[198]

The Washington Public School at Ninth and Carpenter Streets had 1,250 children attending in 1901, and almost all were Italian. They were learning citizenship and English, and to show support for their efforts, C.C.A. offered them ten prizes. The *Inquirer* reported the names of the ten children but noted that one prize went to "William Miller, the only American winner."[199] What the prizes were was not reported. A few months later, teachers at the Washington School were invited to C.C.A.'s home in Roxborough, where they were entertained as a way of thanking them for their efforts.[200]

Ten years later, C.C.A.'s interest in encouraging education for illiterate Italians had a base in South Philadelphia's Washington Public School. A special evening course was created between the American Civic League for the Protection of Immigrants and the city's Board of Education. The news article noted that "C.C.A. Baldi will be in charge."[201]

The apex of recognition for his support of education came in 1924, when a vacancy on the Philadelphia School Board was filled by C.C.A. Beside his photo were his words of appreciation:

"To me the appointment is a challenge for service and I will do my utmost to make good," he said. "Since coming to this country I have had two hobbies, education and Americanization. I have always been eager to enhance these subjects in the minds of foreign-born. Both of these can be obtained from American institutions and a thorough study of the Constitution." [202]

He was sworn in on October 14, ten days later.

C.C.A. Baldi and his wife, as well as their daughter Louise; her husband, Charles G. Douglas; and their three children, all lived on Green Lane in Roxborough next to Manayunk in northwest Philadelphia. The nearby Joel Cook School at Green Lane and Manayunk Avenue was criticized by a parents' group as being a danger to its students because "the sanitary conditions are primitive and endanger the lives of the children." [203]

Not one to look the other way, school board member C.C.A. Baldi said, "That school is a disgrace" and "it is an outrage that such conditions are permitted to exist." [204] He then said that with smallpox breaking out, the lives of the children were at risk. [205]

As for teaching itself, the profession was overwhelmingly female one hundred years ago because the best and the brightest women were not allowed to be doctors, lawyers or upper management, but they could teach and be nurses. Stepping into the thicket of young versus older women, C.C.A. came down on the side of experience. An article in the *Inquirer* was headlined "Older Teachers Urged by Baldi":

"What does a young woman know of life and children?" said Mr. Baldi, in discussing cases of this sort that are before the board. "She may know all the new-fangled ideas about teachers' methods, yes, but she has not the mellowness and serenity in dealing with children the wide experience of the older woman has given her."

Experience an Asset

"When a woman of let us say fifty or yes, even sixty, has taught before her marriage, gone through the great experience of marriage and raising children and is still in good health, she has a store of ripened experience that is invaluable. This experience should be an asset to her, not a liability. Women should not be penalized for leaving the school service for wider spheres of life and not allowed to return with the fruits of their experience to add to the lives of their pupils."

Experienced teachers of sixty or over who have left the service for a time and want to return make better instructors for children than do young inexperienced women asserts C.C.A. Baldi, member of the School Board, and should be allowed to teach in the schools of Philadelphia.[206]

The newspaper editorialized in support of his position, noting:

Should Elders Teach Our Youth?

There is something peculiarly appealing in the argument of C.C.A. Baldi of the Board of Education that we should employ more "elders" for the teaching of American youth. Mr. Baldi presents a thoroughly sensible and well-founded case for age against youth, although there may be many, perhaps, to scoff at his reasoning.

The teaching of youth was very largely in the hands of the elders in ancient times. That is the point from which Mr. Baldi begins his case. The elders had a mass of experience and lore of all kinds accumulated during a lifetime which made them the most valuable repositories of learning in their communities. Youth found them the best teachers, and in its day of old age had an additional accumulation of experience and information to impart.[207]

As for his own children, C.C.A. Baldi pushed education as a key to advancement and an end in and of itself. Sons Joseph and Carmen became lawyers, Frederick a doctor and daughter Louise graduated from the Hill School in Pottstown, Pennsylvania, and for years ran a Presbyterian home for the aged in Bala. My father was Louise Baldi Douglas's firstborn in 1915. His parents later wanted him to go to a prep school, but C.C.A. said that because he was on the school board, his grandchildren would have to go to public school. The solution was a simple one: build a new high school to take care of the Roxborough students.

The boutique high school was opened in 1922. When my father, Charles G. Douglas, Jr., graduated in 1933, there were only fifty-five men and women in his class. All were white. His sister Louise graduated in 1934 and Rose in 1938. Today, the demographics have changed to 91 percent minority, and 100 percent of all the hundreds of students are economically disadvantaged.

C.C.A. Baldi's interest in education also included a desire for his Italian newcomers to be Americanized rather than maintain a separate identity. To strengthen American institutions and to reduce fraud, banking abuse

Roxborough High School. *Author's collection.*

and blackmailers, some of Philadelphia's most prominent men formed a group in 1910, named the North American Civic League for Immigrants.[208] Among the business and civic leaders were famous department store owner John Wanamaker; John H. Converse, president of the massive Baldwin Locomotive Works; and C.C.A. Baldi. Because 90 percent of the immigrants coming to the city did not speak English, they were being taken advantage of. Thus, the goal of the Civic League[209] was to teach economics to the newcomers and show them how to protect themselves from fraud.

By January 1911, "The formal opening of the special evening lecture series for adult aliens" was conducted by Philadelphia's Board of Education in cooperation with the Civic League at the Washington School in South Philadelphia, with C.C.A. Baldi "in charge."[210] The Monday evening series was in Italian. Other nights were at other schools in German, Yiddish and Polish, depending on the neighborhood.

In March 1911, Italian art was on display at Wanamaker's Department Store to celebrate the Golden Jubilee of that business and as a way to congratulate the business. An ad, paid for by C.C.A. Baldi, recognized Wanamaker's as a success for those who come to America and "practice the business principles of strict honesty and industry."[211]

In April 1911, the Italian Beneficial Association of Bristol, Pennsylvania, celebrated its sixth anniversary with a parade and a dinner. The guests of honor included C.C.A. Baldi and Joseph F.M. Baldi. City Councilman Joseph Grundy told the crowd to learn American history and assimilate "the underlying principles upon which the country has been reared."[212] In turn, C.C.A., in Italian, praised Grundy for being a true friend of the Italian community. In keeping with his advocacy for teaching American civics principles, C.C.A. also went to Bridgeport, Connecticut, at the invitation of its mayor to speak to "a gathering of Italians" on "Republican Principles in the United States Government."[213]

In the final year of World War I, on July 4, 1918, delegates from twenty-four nationalities pledged their support of America with a clever replica of the Declaration of Independence worded as a condemnation of the German emperor rather than King George, III. The one-hundred-plus Philadelphia signatories were from Armenia, France, Poland, Italy and more, and on behalf of their nationalities "and on behalf of all the peoples of the earth who love freedom," they pledged "their loyalty and allegiance to the cause of the United States and her Allies." The five Italian American signatories include C.C.A. Baldi and his newspaper rival A. Giuseppe Di Silvestro of *La Libera Parola*.

After World War I, in 1919, many prominent people in Wilmington, Delaware, gathered at the Hotel du Pont at an event to honor Italian military officers:

> *Chevalier C.C.A. Baldi spoke in both English and Italian. He told the Italian citizens that they should show unfailing loyalty to the country of their adoption, America, but they should not forget the love of their mother country, Italy. He said that his reception in America was the kind that a man loves when he is away from his home and family.*[214]

A year later in Wilmington, several hundred people turned out to honor Dr. Leopold Vaccaro, who, like C.C.A., was decorated with the title of chevalier of the Order of the Crown of Italy.[215]

As the first to speak, C.C.A. Baldi said:

> *The Italian inhabitants of Wilmington were 100 per cent American as, in fact are all the Italians who have adopted this country as their home. He added that if they were Republicans so much the better. Continuing, Chevalier Baldi said that no man could be successful unless he had a good wife to back him up and that no man, no matter how many friends he might have, could never hope to be successful if he lost respect for his parents. Likewise no man could be successful if he lost respect for his mother country. Not only would he lose the respect of the people of his mother country, but he would also lose the respect of the people of his adopted country.*[216]

The other Wilmington newspaper said that C.C.A. had praised Dr. Vaccaro for his work Americanizing the Italians in Wilmington. C.C.A. said to hearty applause that he was an "American first and a Republican next," and he then completed his speech in English.[217]

To wipe out illiteracy and to carry out a citywide program of naturalization, the Philadelphia Chamber of Commerce appointed ten men to serve on its Americanization Committee. C.C.A. Baldi was the member on behalf of the Italian community.[218]

In 1921, the Philadelphia *Evening Public Journal* for March 28 ran an editorial by C.C.A. Baldi on what his work for Americanization of Italians meant; it is set forth at the end of this chapter so the reader can see his views at length.

To honor his service and interest in education, the Philadelphia School Board on March 31, 1976, laid the cornerstone for the C.C.A. Baldi Middle School in Northeast Philadelphia. In a handout titled "Who Was C.C.A. Baldi?" the school repeated his words:

> *He said on his appointment to the Philadelphia Board of Education in 1924, "Since coming to this country, I have had two hobbies: Education and Americanization. I have always been eager to imbue these subjects in the minds of foreign-born. Both can be obtained from American institutions and thorough study of the Constitution."*

C.C.A. Baldi Middle School. *School district photo.*

Charles Carmine Antonio Baldi, the first Italian named to the School Board, served on that board until his death in 1930. All Americans take pride in him. He was as true a Philadelphian as William Penn or Benjamin Franklin.

The school is fed by four elementary schools. For grades six through eight, the international flavor has changed from the Philadelphia of the 1920s. As the school said in 1976:

As you walk through our hallways you hear the voices of the world. We are Russian and we are Indian. We are Asian and American. We are white and we are African American and we can hear and we are hearing impaired. We have strengths and we have weaknesses. It is this diversity that makes the C.C.A. Baldi Middle School unique, and it is this same diversity that makes us strong. We are a community of learners; each student striving to succeed in a school that has come to reflect our world.

Editorial by C.C.A. Baldi on Americanization, May 1925

As a blind man needs light, just so do we need Americanization, in the opinion of C.C.A. Baldi, banker and prominent Italian of this city.

Peace, which right now is a vital requisite of this nation, as well as of every nation, can be best gained according to Mr. Baldi, by inculcating that peace into minds which are restless and irritated and ready, at a moment's notice, to flame up in opposition to law and order.

"Americanization," says Mr. Baldi, "I regard as the best method of attaining that general happiness which means success to this great country. No man can do proper justice to himself and to the public in general who is not in accord with the spirit of Americanization.

"By interesting ourselves in this thing that we call Americanization, and which includes many and varied phases, we make our own lives happy, we benefit our homes, we absorb obedience to law, we aid and encourage others in the search for happiness. By practicing the spirit of Americanization, the foreign-born resident secures the confidence and good will of Americans, and he soon becomes an American himself in fact as well as in theory, thereby obtaining all the privileges and advantages which each individual state, and the nation as a unit, offer him.

"What is wealth to a resident of this republic if he has not the privileges of the free-born and the approving consideration of his fellow men? What is a profession worth if he has not the same rights that other men possess? A criminal may make $10,000 or even $1,000,000 by a single nefarious operation, but he is continually haunted and oppressed by the shadow of the law, whereas the honest man who has earned his right to what he possesses has the respect and love of his friends and associates and can hold up his head confidently and proudly without a fear."

True American Wins Respect

"Just so the true American who is faithful and loyal in word and deed to the country of his adoption, possesses peace of mind and the respect of other people, while the man who tries to serve two masters, or lives only for his own selfish interests, is continually distraught and unhappy and discontented.

"Because an Italian or Frenchman or a visitor from some other land is loyal to the United States does not mean, as some other people have claimed, that he is disloyal to his native country. On the contrary he is a credit both to us and his own native land. If he commits a crime, people say, 'Oh, yes, he's an Italian.' Or 'He's a German,' and it is equally true that if he is honest and successful those same people make the same remarks. Thus the man's native country gets the credit or discredit, as the case may be.

"If the immigrant coming here has no intention of adapting himself to the customs and spirit of our country, we do not want him: he might better stay on the other side of the Atlantic. It is just as if a guest in a home insulted and disregarded the wishes or arrangements of his host, only in this case the host is not an individual, but an entire people.

"America has everything that any other nation in the world has and more, and yet a great many foreigners are forever comparing this country unfavorably with their own birthplaces. It is perfectly right for them to leave the latter and to wish to return to visit but they should learn to revere and love their new home and give it implicit and unquestioning loyalty. And so, after all, he can serve two masters, but in such a way to make his loyalty to his adopted country stand as a credit to his native land."

Peace Needed Most of All

"Right at this particular time, what we need most of all is peace. We have shown in the recent war what we might have, but now we must have peace and a contentment of mind. It is an unfortunate fact that certain forms of industrial unrest and trouble we must always have. What we do want is to prevent more of those who might foster such unrest from ever leaving their own countries to bring the trouble to our land.

"Americanization is the best thing that this country has undertaken to remedy whatever faults there are in our present relationships. The American who does not take part in this campaign or is not interested in it is doing as much harm and is often just as dangerous as the man who needs to have inculcated in him this American spirit.

"The whole plan cannot be accomplished by one or a few people; by one political party; by one religious sect; by one portion of the people. It is something that must be united in by everyone, regardless of whether he is Socialist, Republican, Democrat, Catholic, Jew or Protestant.

"It is the root of progress in this nation, and probably the only thing that will bring us up to that standard we are entitled to have. It must be shared by all, from the Chief Executive of our government to the humblest man in the country. The common good of all will be served by a general devotion to the practices and principles of Americanization."

CHAPTER 14

FROM COMMUNITY LEADER
TO KNIGHTHOOD

s early as 1892, when he was only thirty years old, C.C.A. Baldi was the leader of the 400th anniversary parade through the city for Columbus's landing in the New World.[219] My father, as a child, remembered seeing C.C.A. on a white horse leading the annual Columbus Day parades.

As business after business was formed by the Baldi brothers, C.C.A. became both a community and political leader. After a summer trip to Italy in 1902, he obviously planted an article remarking on how all over Naples the people were wearing "Pennypacker for Governor" buttons. C.C.A. had taken "a large quantity" of the buttons and given them to friends and associates "as small tokens of his esteem and as symbols of America's greatness."[220] Republican Samuel Pennypacker won and served as governor of Pennsylvania from 1903 to 1907.

Upon C.C.A.'s return from his trip, over one hundred prominent Italians, including court interpreter Emmanuel V.H. Nardi as toastmaster, held a testimonial dinner for him.[221]

Italian Community Celebrates Return of Banker
from His Trip Abroad

There was an imposing turn out of residents in the Italian community yesterday morning, to celebrate the return of Charles C.A. Baldi, the well-known banker at 928 South Eighth street, who has spent the summer in Italy. There was a parade by the San Biagio Society, of which Mr. Baldi is president, and, later in the day, a picnic was held in Washington Park, numerous Italian societies participating.

His trip was not entirely one of pleasure. A project has been formed by prominent Italian citizens here to place in Fairmount Park a series of monuments of their distinguished countrymen. It is proposed to erect first a monument to the great composer Verdi and then another to Christopher Columbus. While abroad Mr. Baldi made a careful study of the subject, visiting some of the most famous Italian sculptors and the monument movement among his countrymen in this city will probably take shape in a short time.

Efforts will be made to interest Italians throughout the city in the project. Already assurances have been given of liberal contributions from leading members of the no less than fifty prosperous organizations that are enrolled under the banner of the United Italian Societies.[222]

After that same trip, C.C.A. was able to announce that Italy's justice minister had agreed to serve as honorary president of the St. Biagio Society in South Philadelphia. The society's president was C.C.A., and he was given a "handsome silver loving cup in memory of his return from abroad."[223]

In 1903, Pope Leo XIII died, and "Little Italy Bows Its Head in Silent Sorrow for Pope" was the *Inquirer* headline for July 29.[224] The *Inquirer* reported that prior to a requiem mass at Our Lady of Good Counsel Church, "the entire colony seemed to have congregated about Eighth and Christian Streets."[225] The grand marshal for the solemn ceremonies was C.C.A. Baldi. Over fifty Italian societies participated.[226]

Two years later, on September 8, 1905, a 7.1-magnitude earthquake struck Calabria in southern Italy, killing hundreds and leveling many towns and villages. The folks in Philadelphia's Little Italy sprang into action to raise money for their *paesanos*. What was described as "a monster parade"[227] was scheduled for two days made up of more than five thousand Italians and one hundred societies marching from South Philadelphia to the center of the city. Collecting money from the crowd of onlookers "will be six carriages containing twenty-four girls, the most beautiful that can be found in the Italian quarter."[228] Not surprisingly, the chief marshal was C.C.A. Baldi. Others in the procession were Count Nasseli, the Italian consul, Father Caruso and Father Isoleri. The goal was to raise $10,000 for the victims in Italy.

In 1907, the Duke of Abruzzi visited Philadelphia as a salute to the Italian community. The duke was an admiral of the Italian navy and a cousin of the

MONEY CAST AT PARADERS TO AID VOLCANO VICTIMS

Volcano victims fundraising in Philadelphia. *From* Philadelphia Inquirer, *September 19, 1905.*

king. C.C.A. Baldi accompanied the duke along with the former ambassador to Italy, William Potter. A reception was held at the Academy of Music in center city.[229] The duke stayed at C.C.A.'s home in Roxborough.[230]

Feast days at the various churches for their patron saints are always colorful events. Statues with streamers are paraded through the streets, and people come forward to pin dollar bills to the streamers. One procession for St. Mary Magdalen de Pazzi was described in the *Inquirer* in June 1907:

> *It is a time honored custom that money shall be pinned upon certain of the statues that are carried in the procession. Again and again the procession is halted while the lines of men and women crowding the curb are broken to give passage to a man or woman who wants to pin a one, two, five or ten-dollar bill upon the statue of a favorite saint.*
>
> *In the home of C.C.A. Baldi, who is one of the leaders among the Italian people in this city, a crowd of the most representative men of Little Italy gathered to watch the procession. There were Mr. Baldi, his brother, Joseph Baldi, Court Interpreter E.V.N. Nardi, Professor Alphonso Rosa,*

Parade of saints. *From Michael di Pilla*, South Philadelphia's Little Italy *(2016)*.

Joseph Lucareni and a host of others. From the window of Mr. Baldi's home they watched the procession go by.

At very short intervals the marchers would stop while a man or woman pinned a bill to the already large streamers floating from the statues. Some of the Italians seemed wild with fervor. The statue of St. Anthony was covered with bills before it had covered a square. Then came the Madonna and Child, also covered with bills.[231]

The same Father Caruso who marched with C.C.A. in the earthquake fundraiser had a falling out with one of his priests at Our Lady of Good Counsel Church. Reverend Nicolo Mucci left the church at Eighth and Christian Streets but didn't have far to go. The press reported he became a clerk in the C.C.A. Baldi & Company coal dealership around the corner.[232] The backstory is unknown, but Father Mucci said, "I do not intend to marry."[233]

A family summer vacation in Cape May, New Jersey, was a place for an event by C.C.A., who was by then a chevalier knighted by the king of Italy. C.C.A. supervised the creation of Italian dishes at the Cape May Yacht Club, with guests including an array of old Philadelphia families with English and German names of origin:

Cav C.C.A. Baldi yesterday gave an Italian dinner at the Cape May Yacht Club at Cape May. His guests were: Commodore J. Clifford Wilson, Vice Commodore Dr. R. Walter Starr, Rear Commodore James F. Lucas, J.F. Jacoby, W.H. McFillen, W.H. Long, Colonel Lewis E. Beiter, Louis J. McGrath, W.M. Stockhausen, B.S. Bunn, H.L. Hunsicker, A.C. Thomas, E.B. Midlen, J.L. Shoemaker, Dr. Howard Kingsbury and Colonel J. Warner Hutchins.[234]

Later in 1908, C.C.A. invited fifty prominent businessmen and city officials through the Italian quarter, visiting churches and businesses on a "Tally Ho Trip" using the funeral home's beautiful coaches.[235] The afternoon ended with a banquet of Italian dishes at 1011 South Eighth Street, the location of the Baldi brothers businesses. Earlier, a fencing contest was held at Pennsylvania Hall, featuring foils and broadswords with the champions of Italy and Germany.[236] The Italian Generoso Pavese was Teddy Roosevelt's fencing coach.

Not too small to be overlooked, C.C.A. Baldi's wife, Louise, was on the reception committee for the fourteenth annual ball to raise money for "Little Italian Orphans."[237]

At the end of 1908, it was back to fundraising for a natural disaster. A December 1908 earthquake hit Calabria with a 7.1 on the Richter scale, and the result was a forty-foot tsunami that leveled the cities of Reggio Calabria and Messina, resulting in seventy-five thousand to eighty-two thousand deaths.

Mayor Reyburn of Philadelphia called a meeting of the Citizens Permanent Relief Committee to plan on sending aid to southern Italy.[238] The Italian Federation—under the lead of C.C.A. Baldi as president and E.V.H. Nardi as treasurer—sprang into action to raise money for the victims.[239] Hundreds of relatives of the quake victims flooded the Italian consulate and the offices of *L'Opinione*.[240] Even famous tenor Enrico Caruso, who performed in the city, donated his $2,500 fee to the cause.[241] The federation located its fundraising headquarters at the offices of C.C.A. Baldi at Eighth and Montrose Streets.[242]

As part of his role as civic leader of Little Italy, C.C.A. was chosen to serve in many capacities as the founder and president of the Italian Federation, a member of the Dante Alighieri Circolo, the Pennsylvania Manufacturers' Club, the Italian Chamber of Commerce, the Pennsylvania Society, the Roxborough Country Club, the Young Republicans, the Improved Order of Red Men and the Big Brothers Association. He also served as honorary vice president of the Academy of Music.[243] His government positions included being a member of the Board of Governors of the Glen Mills Schools, treasurer of the Washington Crossing Park Commission, secretary of the Pennsylvania State Board of Undertakers and a member of the Philadelphia Board of Public Education from 1915 until his death. He also served on the Atlantic Deeper Waterways Convention.

In 1916, Baldi Hall, located at the spacious funeral home, was the site for a sanitation and public health campaign.[244]

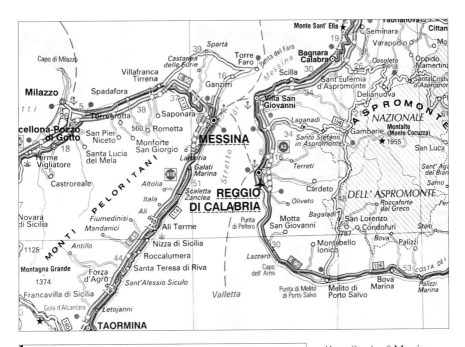

Above: Strait of Messina between Sicily and Calabria, Italy. *ITMB Publishing (public domain)*.

Left: Public health campaign at Baldi Hall. *From* Philadelphia Inquirer, *June 9, 1916*.

TO BOOM HEALTH CAMPAIGN

Big Meeting Downtown Will Launch Welfare Work

To stir the residents of that section of the city between Fitzwater and Ellsworth, Seventh and Twelfth streets, to a deeper interest in their own personal and civic welfare, and to procure their co-operation in matters of public health and sanitation, a public meeting, under the auspices of the Department of Health and Charities and the Child Federation will be held tonight, at Baldi Hall, 1011 South Eighth street.

Chevalier C. C. A. Baldi will preside, and addresses will be made by Director Krusen, of the Department of Health and Charities; Chief John A. Vogleson, of the Bureau of Health; Chief James A. McCrudden, of the Division of Housing and Sanitation, and Dr. Doan, of the Philadelphia General Hospital. The first work to be taken up will be a baby saving campaign.

Sliding boards, tetherball, seesaws and other playground equipment were funded by C.C.A. Baldi in 1916 for the Montrose playground in South Philadelphia. Addressing ceremonies in Italian, C.C.A. said proper recreation areas in the crowded neighborhood "would result later in better citizenship."[245]

Later that year, the Church of St. Nicholas of Tolentino at Ninth and Watkins Streets was dedicated by C.C.A. and a crowd of three thousand.[246]

Lay Church Cornerstone
Bishop McCort Officiates at Ceremony in Italian Section

With Bishop J. McCort Officiating at the impressive ceremony the cornerstone of the new Catholic Church of St. Nicholas of Tolentino, at Ninth and Watkins streets, was laid yesterday afternoon.

The new church, which is of the Rococo style of Roman architecture, and constructed of brick with limestone trimmings, will be ready about February, 1917. It will take the place of the mission established about two years ago by the Augustine Fathers. Rev. Daniel Scallabrella, who has been in charge of the mission, will continue as rector of the new church which was made possible largely through the patronage of Chevalier C.C.A. Baldi. More than three thousand persons attended the ceremonies yesterday.[247]

When the cornerstone for Our Lady of the Eternal Parish was laid in 1927, the bishop, mayor and C.C.A. were there, along with the first Italian judge, Eugene V. Alessandroni. The Italian parish school had sixteen classrooms.[248]

Another celebration occurred when Major General Umberto Nobile, the pilot of Roald Amundsen's airship the *Norge*, came to Philadelphia.[249] Famous polar explorer Amundsen of Norway joined an Italian crew led by Nobile in the airship *Norge*, which crossed the North Pole, leaving from Spitsbergen in May 1926 and landing in Alaska. Prime Minister Benito Mussolini had assumed power in Italy in 1922 as the head of the National Fascist Party; thus, the salute of the *fascisti* was for Nobile. Thousands turned out to cheer the general, with C.C.A. at his side.[250]

In addition to civic activities for the Italian community at large, C.C.A. also sought to help those he considered wrongfully accused. Twenty-nine-year-old Antonio Taddai and his friend Giovani Macuri were in Reading, Pennsylvania, on July 4, 1902, playing a street organ and collecting small change. Three men followed them up and down various streets, harassing

NORGE PILOT VISITS PHILADELPHIA

SALUTE OF FASCISTI STIRS NORGE PILOT AS HE VISITS PHILA.

"Vivas" for Hero and for Rome Greet General Nobile

Police Have Difficulty in Hazing Back Thousands Eger to See Navigator

By RICHARD J. BEAMISH

MRS. HALL AT HOME | UNDERWORLD LORDS

A famous pilot visits Philadelphia. *From* Philadelphia Inquirer, *July 18, 1926.*

the two Italians. One man said, "This time we'll kill the damned Italians." Another man knocked Taddai down, causing a head cut after jumping the organ grinder from behind. Prior to this, a witness said the trio were throwing large firecrackers at the two musicians. One of the three men said he wanted to fight Taddai and was "not afraid of all their [Italian] knives."[251] Fortunately, Taddai had been in America long enough to have a gun, which he pulled out of a pocket, shooting and killing all three of his tormentors.

Indicted for murder, young Taddai sat in court five months later with C.C.A. Baldi, who paid lawyers for his defense. After getting the case, the jury in Berks County came back with a not guilty verdict.[252] The jurors included farmers and tradesmen with largely German names like Dietrich, Kniebel, Dengler and Frauenfelder. When asked if Taddai would resume his life as a street musician, C.C.A. said, "No, he will be going into his coal business."[253]

Four years later, in 1906, Governor Pennypacker, whom C.C.A. had supported strongly, recalled a death warrant for the execution of Carmen Renzo in Indiana County, Pennsylvania. The hanging was indefinitely postponed after a petition was filed on behalf of the Italian Federation of the City of Philadelphia by its president, C.C.A. Baldi.

As she knew he was always ready to help a victim of domestic abuse, Nellie Lista turned to C.C.A. after killing her husband following a beating he gave her. Louis Lista was a drunk who had twice before been arrested for assaulting Nellie, who was the main support for a large number of children. When Louis beat her on July 13, 1915, Nellie took a butcher knife to defend herself and stabbed Louis. The next day, she went to C.C.A.'s office before she would surrender to the police.[254] He arranged with the authorities to have her taken into custody, and then he posted bond for her in the amount of $2,500 so she could get out of jail.[255]

An early proponent of the war on drugs, C.C.A. and his brother Joseph F.M. Baldi joined with police to round up young men selling cocaine "in the crusade being made against the sellers and users of the drug."[256] Eight were arrested.

In 1907, because of his many contributions to the Italian colony in Philadelphia, C.C.A. Baldi was made a cavaliere or chevalier of the Order of the Crown of Italy by King Victor Emmanuel, III. The April 19, 1907 letter of award appears in the appendix. A man by the name of H.M. Jacobi drafted an aristocratic sonnet to the new knight, which is also in the appendix, along with a translation from Italian. The *Inquirer* offered its congratulations as follows:

C.C.A. wearing the medal of a chevalier, November 1907. *Author's collection.*

Congratulations to C.C.A. Baldi, "the King of Little Italy," on his recognition by the King of Greater Italy. With all his dignities he is a good American citizen.[257]

A "big banquet to their distinguished leader" was held on May 30, 1907, at Beneficial Hall to honor C.C.A. on his knighthood. City politicians and Italian leaders, including Court Interpreter, Emmanuel V. H. Nardi, gathered to congratulate him.[258]

Twelve years later, the king also conferred the military title of commander or *commendatore*, on C.C.A., who had served in the Italian army in the 1870s.[259]

CHAPTER 15

THE VARE AND BALDI REPUBLICAN PARTY MACHINE

P rior to C.C.A. Baldi's death in 1930, his alliance with the boss of Philadelphia's controlling Republican political party was a source of great power in South Philadelphia's "river wards." Boss William Scott Vare was a true son of South Philly and grew up on a pig and produce farm at Fourth Street and Snyder Avenue. His two older brothers were George and Edwin, and the three were known as the "Dukes of South Philadelphia."

Bill's political bug started in 1884, when he watched the Mummer's Day Parade on New Year's Day and realized such marches could be employed in political campaigns.

The Vare brothers started a family business hauling ash and garbage in South Philadelphia. In 1890, Bill started construction contracting with his two older brothers. Vare Brothers Contracting worked on excavating, paving and municipal contracts for the City of Philadelphia that totaled $7 million between 1909 and 1912. Their projects included building trolley tracks, sewers, the Municipal Stadium and the Broad Street subway and excavating the site of the Philadelphia Art Museum. Vare was elected to the Philadelphia City Council in 1898 and served until 1901.

The Republican Party had controlled Philadelphia for decades, but a reform group split off and formed the Union Party. The GOP machine split gave Bill Vare his chance to seize power. In his words:

South Philadelphia having been ignored, or at least neglected, for decades by the Republican leaders of the city, it was early determined to give a resident of that section the nomination for an important county office.

> *The Vares, as the leading factors of the district in support of the new Republican Organization regime, were conceded the place for the South Philadelphia section, and Durham and Boies Penrose urged that I be named Recorder of Deeds.*[260]

Vare served as recorder of deeds from 1902 to 1912, when he was elected to the State Senate and the U.S. House of Representatives at the same time. He served seven terms in the House. William Vare even won a seat in the U.S. Senate in 1926 but was never seated due to widespread allegations of corruption and voter fraud.

The pandemic Spanish flu took a high toll in Philadelphia because its public health response was weak and disorganized. J. Barry, author of *The Great Influenza*, singled out Philadelphia's crowding and lack of services, even compared to New York's Tammany Hall Machine:

> *All this made Philadelphia fertile ground for epidemic disease. So did a city government incapable of responding to a crisis. Muckraker Lincoln Steffens called Philadelphia "the worst-governed city in America." He may well have been right.*
>
> *Even Tammany's use of power in New York was haphazard compared to that of the Philadelphia machine, which had returned to power in 1916 after a reformer's single term in office. Philadelphia's boss was Republican state senator Edwin Vare. He had bested and mocked people who considered themselves his betters, people who despised him, people with such names as Wharton, Biddle, and Wanamaker.*[261]

All city workers kicked back a portion of their salary to the Vare machine. To be sure that no one missed a payment, they were paid not at city hall but across the street at GOP headquarters. The mayor's kickback was $1,000. As for the weak opposition Democrats, their chairman, John O'Donnell, was on the Republican payroll, and the Vares even paid the rent for the Democratic Party's headquarters.[262]

> *State Senator Edwin Vare was also the city's biggest contractor, and his biggest contract was for street cleaning, a contract he had held for almost twenty years. At a time when a family could live in comfort on $3,000 a year, in 1917 he had received over $5 million for the job. Not all of that money stayed in Vare's pockets, but even the part that left passed through them and paid a toll. Yet the streets were notoriously filthy, especially in*

South Philadelphia—where the need was greatest, where everything but raw sewage, and sometimes even that, ran through the gutters, and where the machine was strongest.

Ironically, the very lack of city services strengthened the machine since it provided what the city did not: food baskets to the poor, help with jobs and favors, and help with the police—the commissioner and many magistrates were in Vare's pocket.[263]

After Ed's death in 1922, the baton passed to William until his death in 1934. Violence was part of the Vare machine's playbook if needed:

On primary election day in 1917, several Vare workers blackjacked two leaders of an opposing faction, then beat to death a policeman who intervened. The incident outraged the city. Vare's chief lieutenant in 1918 was Mayor Thomas B. Smith. In his one term in office he would be indicted, although acquitted, on three entirely unrelated charges, including conspiracy to murder that policeman. That same election, however, gave Vare absolute control over both the Select and Common Councils, the city's legislature, and broad influence in the state legislature.[264]

The key to jobs for votes were jobs as street cleaners. Immigrant Italians had no skills for an urban city and were largely illiterate. They thus gravitated to labor and construction jobs. As Professor Luconi describes it:

Through the brokerage of Charles C.A. Baldi Sr., the almost unchallenged political leader of his fellow ethnics until his death in 1930, Vare's organization supplied the unemployed with jobs in the city and county administrations, provided the destitute with free clothing and baskets of food on major holidays, and helped people in trouble with the law. In particular, the Republican machine had given Philadelphians of Italian descent a virtual monopoly on street cleaning positions since the late nineteenth century. In 1914, for instance, Philadelphia had nearly 1,600 street sweepers. They were almost exclusively of Calabrian and Sicilian ancestry. The GOP was also instrumental in granting Italian Americans jobs in the U.S. Navy yard.[265]

In 1911, William Vare spoke to a large gathering of Italians at Eighth and Christian Streets on behalf of his candidate for mayor. Vare refuted charges that the street cleaners had not had their wages raised. He said as a candidate for recorder of deeds he stood for "the plain, common people."[266] Others addressing the meeting were C.C.A. and Joseph Baldi.[267]

The Vare machine needed the Baldis, and vice versa, because C.C.A.

> *knew that he had what the Vare machine needed: a capacity to function as a trusted intermediary between the growing immigrant community and the external political society. Baldi ensured the Italian votes for Vare, who reciprocated with jobs and favors, thus assisting Baldi in his own dynastic ambitions....*
>
> *Frequently these relationships were unsavory, yet even so they stemmed from the necessities of urban political life. Like immigrant bosses elsewhere, the opportunistic Baldi had seized the chance to command the ethnic community, thus consummating a strategic alliance with the existing power bloc.[268]*

The Vares' technique had been well summarized by Edwin Vare as simply: "Take care of your people and your people will take care of you."[269] Professor Varbero recounts that C.C.A. would stand at the door of the bank on Eighth Street and hand out dollar bills to the needy.[270] C.C.A. also had Saturday morning request time on his front porch at his Green Lane residence in Roxborough, where his people could come ask for help with housing, food, a job or whatever was troubling them. The bombing of the house (see chapter 17) was on that porch, seen on the facing page.

Of course, power came C.C.A.'s way because of his sway as "King of Little Italy." "C.C.A. Baldi ruled Little Italy, and everyone who wished to deal with the Italians knew it. His near absolute control of the Italian vote in the downtown wards thus secured for him the political patronage and honorifics due to such a powerful Republican."[271]

In 1920, Italian Americans were the second-largest nationality group in Philadelphia at 182,368.[272] Despite this size, it was New York that elected Fiorello La Guardia as mayor in 1934. South Philadelphia–born (1920) Francis Rizzo did not become the first Italian American mayor of Philadelphia until 1972. Frank Rizzo served until 1980, and his plaque in South Philadelphia commemorates his reign. A Republican, Rizzo was police commissioner and then ran for mayor as a Democrat but reverted to the GOP in 1986.

For their numbers, the community was also underrepresented in the state legislature:

Louisa S. Baldi and five of her children. *Author's collection.*

By 1919 there were two Philadelphia Italian legislators in the State House of Representatives. C.C.A. Baldi, Jr., an organization Republican, won his seat in the Second District (Second Ward) in 1917. Since the elder Baldi maintained absolute control of that ward, his son held the seat consistently into the 1930s. In 1919 Nicolas DiLemmo was elected from the Third District on the Republican slate. DiLemmo, however, did not win re-election. It is noteworthy that Baldi was not rejoined by a fellow Philadelphia Italian until 1929, when Biagio Cantania, a Democrat representing the First District (First Ward), rode the Al Smith wave to the state legislature. Catania also failed to repeat, however. In 1930 Giuseppe Argentieri, an organization Republican, took a seat representing the Fifth District which was the Vare's 26th Ward.[273]

Teaming up the thousands of Italian voters in Baldi's Second and Vare's Twenty-Sixth Wards all went well for the GOP until 1928, when the Democratic National Party nominated Governor Al Smith of New York for president. He had two strong appeals to Italians: he was a Roman Catholic, and he opposed the immigration quotas that Congress had enacted a few years earlier. In 1928, Vare's Twenty-Sixth Ward had 19,995 registered voters, and 70 percent were Italian.[274] For the first time in memory, the Twenty-Sixth voted Democratic with Smith over Herbert Hoover, 11,405 to 7,913.[275] Also a factor was Vare's support of liquor as a "wet," while Hoover was a "dry."[276]

The Democratic upheaval was blunted in the Second Ward due to an all-out Baldi and *L'Opinione* push:

The Second Ward, C.C.A. Baldi's territory, brought less success for Smith supporters. Here in the very heart of Little Italy the Baldi family campaigned energetically for Hoover. C.C.A. Baldi, Jr., argued quite logically that "Italians know...Smith's election will not turn on the beer spigots and that Governor Smith himself cannot rearrange the immigration quotas." The elder Baldi and his son Vito, as well as C.C.A., Jr., conducted an extensive "re-education" campaign among Italian-Americans. The results were positive for the Baldi leadership. The Second Ward remained loyal, downing Smith, 2,755 to 2,671.

In fact, none of the Little Italy wards—Two, Three, and Four—gave victories to Smith.[277]

The dramatic election changes came from an energized group named the Philadelphia Italian Democratic Committee, headed by John Crisconi,

Michael Spatola and Joseph Tumolillo and aided by attorney Joseph Marinelli. In Little Italy at St. Paul's Hall, Marinelli and Tumolillo attacked Vare in Italian for being of the party "responsible for discrimination against Italians in the immigration quota" that would do nothing to help "in bringing our mothers and brothers to this country."[278]

Running as a reform Republican for governor in 1930 was Gifford Pinchot, who in an earlier term as governor had fired C.C.A. If all politics is personal, then this race certainly was.

> *The regular Italians loyal to Baldi could have had little love for Pinchot.... C.C.A. Baldi, Sr., had engaged in a bitter public exchange with Pinchot in 1925, after the governor had dismissed Baldi from the State Board of Undertakers. Pinchot described Baldi as a "destructive influence" and characterized his attitude as "abusive and intolerable." More likely, Baldi's close political relationship with Vare had offended Pinchot because Baldi had served on the Board for twelve years without controversy. The old Italian leader countered with a letter indicting Pinchot's policies. But revenge was postponed until the gubernatorial campaign of 1930. Pinchot won statewide but lost in Philadelphia. The governor-elect received only 109 votes in Baldi's Second Ward.[279]*

For the 1930 election, the machine went into high gear after the Al Smith scare. A rump Republican group called the Independents had an Italian named Thomas Descano as its leader and appealed to the Al Smith Italians to repudiate the Vare-Baldi machine and reform the city.

> *Countering the independent Republican threats were solid organization men holding out the promise of jobs. In a declining job market, the workers could not help but be practical. A 26th Ward Leader bragged about his success "at City Hall in getting jobs for men aiding the ticket." The politico was frank: "I got nine places this week and while they pay only $25 to $28 a week, there is nothing laborious about them." Independents could not dispense jobs on equal terms with the machine. Ultimately, any Smith euphoria evaporated in the face of economic depression and trusted organization techniques.[280]*

In the 1932 presidential election, Wards One through Five in Little Italy increased the vote for Hoover by a small margin, but the Democratic vote declined.[281]

Wards 2 and 26 Votes[eeeeeee]

	1928 Smith (D)	1928 Hoover (R)	1932 Roosevelt (D)	1932 Hoover (R)
Ward Two (Baldi)	2,822	3,848	1,989	4,479
Ward Twenty-Six (Vare)	11,405	7,913	10,310	7,281

C.C.A. Baldi died in 1930 after the November election, but a move to a two-party system had begun. Professor Varbero says the slow rise of Italian politicians in Philadelphia thereafter was due to a decline of leadership from the level of the 1920s.[282]

The demise of Italian leadership can be illustrated by the fact that neither C.C.A. Baldi nor A. Giuseppe Di Silvestro was replaced after he died. The deaths of the key first-generation leaders within a brief period (1927–1930) marked the end of Italian political adjustment. As ethnic group spokesmen, each immigrant leader was highly talented and successful, Baldi, perhaps, particularly so.[283]

However, successful though he was, "Baldi was limited by his immigrant background and lack of formal schooling. He never mastered English sufficiently to enable him to address American audiences. Nor was he able to escape entirely his early role as *padrone*. Much like Vare, he mastered urban politics for his own ends."[284]

CHAPTER 16

CRITICS AND RIVALS

With power and influence, it is natural there would be critics, opponents and rivals for C.C.A. Baldi. Professor Varbero saw style and class differences in the Italian community:

> *Some middle class activists were embittered by Baldi's rule, not the least because he had eclipsed their own leadership pretensions. Nevertheless, the middle class Italian reformers shared Baldi's aspirations for the city's immigrants, although their motives were far less materialistic. As a rule, they were much less skillful in the arena of ward politics: they continued to exercise the rhetoric of reform in vain.* [285]

Opposition from reformers was also tied to the Vare machine's interlock with the Baldis:

> *In the face of criticism, the machine powers were not obtuse; they were merely indifferent to the reformers. This attitude explains why the middle class and reformist opposition needed every pretext to strike at Baldi. The Italian champions of reform were too few, too insular, too remote from the ethnic community. The anti-machine element thus advanced seemingly irrelevant arguments for political change, and the Vare-Baldi alignment smiled at its opponent's vulnerability.* [286]

C.C.A.'s more educated antagonists included the brothers Giovanni and A. Giuseppe Di Silvestro, Dr. Leopold Vaccaro and attorney (later judge) Eugene V. Alessandroni. While they were critical of C.C.A., they often publicly appeared together at events where Italians had to present a united front.[287]

There were also the rival newspaper differences because the Di Silvestros took the former *La Voce del Popolo* and turned it into their weekly *La Libera Parola* to challenge *L'Opinione*.[288] The brothers were crusading liberals, while the Baldis were conservative Republicans, with *L'Opinione* as a daily newspaper having the advantage.[289]

> *Other small factions also opposed the Republican status quo and targeted the Baldi family. Early in 1917* La Ragione *appeared, a short-lived weekly conceived as an "organ in defense of Italianity." At the outset it pointedly disavowed any connections with the existing anti-Baldi wing led by the Di Silvestros. In one issue the paper announced, quite erroneously, that the entire colony of 160,000 Italians in Philadelphia repudiated the leadership of Baldi and his son Vito.*[290]

Splits in the Italian societies also arose out of rivalries. The Di Silvestros were prominent figures in the Order of the Sons of Italy, while C.C.A. was head of the Italian Federation of Philadelphia. They were all Republicans despite their other differences. While the Sons of Italy was formally a nonpartisan organization, the leadership of the Pennsylvania Grand Lodge was connected to the Republican Party. Giovanni Di Silvestro was the national head of the Sons of Italy from 1922 through 1935.[291] In 1923, attorney Eugene V. Alessandroni replaced A. Giuseppe Di Silvestro as grand venerable of the lodge and evolved into part of the Vare machine. Alessandroni became the first Italian judge in Philadelphia in 1927, when he was elected to the Court of Common Pleas.[292]

Another split came during the tragedy of loss of life in Italy in the 1906 eruption of Mount Vesuvius. The Di Silvestros and C.C.A.

> *struggled over the issue of who was entitled to represent Philadelphia's community in the collection of funds and could, hopefully, enjoy the rewards of that charitable action in the eyes of its rank and file members. Similarly, a delay in the dedication of Verdi's monument paved the way for innuendoes that Baldi had embezzled the money of other donors.*[293]

Judge Eugene V. Alessandroni. *Philadelphia Bar Association.*

An important Italian association of professionals and businessmen named the Circolo Italiano had a blow-up in 1917 and split into the Baldi and Di Silvestro factions. The catalyst was an alleged slight to the Italian community that revolved around the elder Baldi's narrow selection of "respectables" for presentation to Mayor Thomas B. Smith; Baldi had excluded his political opponents from the list. Since an invitation—in this case to an honor banquet for the Italian diplomatic missions—conveyed community prestige, the excluded Italians were incensed. The Baldi clan had struck "a mortal blow to the Italian colony," since they had selected only representatives from their own faction.[294]

Among those who signed one letter in 1918 denouncing Baldi as an "enemy of the Italians of Philadelphia" were Robert Lombardi, a fast-rising contractor; Eugene V. Alessandroni, the prominent young lawyer soon to be named assistant district attorney; Francis A. Travascio, an Italian undertaker highly prominent and active in professional circles; Reverend Tomasso della Cioppa; and Antonio Veglione, an activist in fraternal orders.[295]

The Circolo Italiano ousted C.C.A. in 1917, when it sponsored an Italian Reconstruction Committee that he opposed.[296] Professor Luconi said that the *prominenti* wanted to show off their Italy-oriented patriotism in their search for status and respect in the community, and this led to the jockeying for position in the Baldi and Di Silvestro camps.[297]

The above battles made it into the newspapers in 1917. In the June 23, 1917 edition of the *Momento* in Philadelphia, the Circolo Italiano resolution was published in full asking for C.C.A. and Vito Baldi to resign, as they were not "in accord with the noble aims and ideals" of the organization.[298] The nub of the problem, according to C.C.A., was that the guest list to dine with the Italian envoys was limited to one hundred people.[299] Of course, one not invited was Joseph (Giuseppe) Di Silvestro, the grand master of the Sons of Italy. In one newspaper account, the anti-Baldi group said C.C.A. was the community's leader "only in his own opinion," and his aim was the promotion of his family "to various political positions to spread his power."[300] After the dust-up, the Italian consul made sure Di Silvestro was included, and C.C.A. was quoted as saying, "They are making a mistake by causing all this fuss."[301]

A week later, salt was rubbed in the wounds when the *Inquirer* ran a story titled "Rare Honor Conferred upon Chevalier Baldi."[302] The story recounted that C.C.A. had received word on July 2 that he was awarded the title of chevalier of the Order of the Crown of Italy. The paper said this was "an honor rarely conferred on residents outside of the mother country."[303] It was given in recognition of his "educational and charitable work for his fellow countrymen in the United States."[304]

Later, the *Inquirer* reported that 250 prominent Italians were counting on July 9, 1917, to create a permanent organization "opposed to Chevalier C.C.A. Baldi."[305] Various society presidents were to be present representing 35,000 members.

In August 1917, a fund of $10,000 was being raised by the Italian Reconstruction Committee "to fight the influence of Chevalier C.C.A.

C. C. A. BALDI DENIES CHARGES OF CRITICS

Declares Personal Enmity Sole Basis for Attacks—Denies He Sligted Countrymen

In a letter addressed to L'Opinione yesterday, Chevalier C. C. A. Baldi, a leader in the Italian colony here, replied to criticism of himself, growing out of the recent visit to Philadelphia of the Royal Italian Commission, and charged that numerous attacks aimed at him have personal enmity for their sole justification.

He denied that he tried, as charged, to prevent the attendance at a dinner given by the city to members of the mission, of the Grand Venerable of the Sons of Italy, nor did he wish to prevent Monsignor Isolari from being asked to speak at the dinner, he said. He also denied he prevented a parade of the lodges of the Sons of Italy, or interfered with the presentation at the dinner of a gold medal for General Cadorna, until a few days ago in supreme command of the Italian armies.

In conclusion Chevalier Baldi asserted his critics and enemies "would like to continue this misrepresentation to accomplish the separation of the forces of our countrymen at a moment when union is so essential for strength and respect."

Left: C.C.A. denies charges by critics. *From* Philadelphia Inquirer, November 18, 1917.

Below: Premier Benito Mussolini. *Wikipedia.*

Baldi as Italian leader" in the city.[306] The reported goal was a mass meeting in October, when plans "will be revealed for the fight to be launched against Baldi's leadership."[307]

C.C.A. pushed back.

A 1922 book passage critical of C.C.A. said:

> *Among the Italians he has passed for a Roman Catholic; in the American residential district where he lives, he is a member of a Protestant church. He has been able to capitalize his reputation, without holding great office, as to be the colonial boss, so that no Italian considered that he could accomplish anything without recourse to his influence. Although evidently his first thought is for himself, he himself really believes that he is giving his life for his people.[308]*

Another point of contention in the Italian community was the rise of Benito Mussolini and Fascism, with most, but not all, being supportive of both. Italy lost one million people in World War I, and after the war came economic disruption with a rise in Communism. In 1922, Benito Mussolini took over Italy, and his followers were numerous in Philadelphia. Il Duce initially received favorable coverage in the American press, and most of the Italian community was proud of what he was doing. In fact, the first Fascist Club was formed in the city in 1921.[309]

> *Prominent local Italian-American leaders like John Di Silvestro and Judge Eugene V. Alessandroni were outspoken admirers of Mussolini, and all the main Italian Language newspapers—*L'Opinione, La Libera Parola, Il Popolo Italiano, *and* Ordine Nuovo—*backed his dictatorship until Italy declared war on the United States.*
>
> *When Dino Grandi, the Minister for Foreign Affairs of the Fascist regime, visited Philadelphia on November 20, 1931, the delegations of 168 Italian-American associations welcomed him at the Baltimore and Ohio Railroad station and a huge crowd greeted him outside. When Mussolini attacked Ethiopia in 1935, Philadelphia's Italian Americans hurried to hold mass rallies to support Italy's bid for an empire, and contributed both their wedding rings and money to finance that colonial war.[310]*

C.C.A. and his brothers supported Mussolini, and *L'Opinione* had a *fascisti* leaning when covering affairs in Italy. But not all in the city were supportive, as will be seen in the next chapter.

At night going to bed, the children of Charles G. Douglas, Jr., and Louise E. Baldi remember her singing a stanza from "Giovinezza," the 1922 official hymn of the Italian National Fascist Party: *Giovinezza, giovinezza primavera di bellezza nel fascismo e la salvezza della nostra libertà*. The translation is, "Youth, youth, spring of beauty in fascism is the salvation of our liberty."

Despite his critics and political opponents, when C.C.A. died, the *Public Ledger* said that the battles discussed previously "had little effect on his standing in the community, as he remained until his death the best known and best loved man of his race."[311]

CHAPTER 17

ATTEMPTED ASSASSINATION
BY BOMBING

At the turn of the twentieth century, there was an increase in Bolshevik and Anarchist Red activity in Italy, Europe and America. As early as 1904, an attack was made on a religious procession of the Feast of St. Mary Magdalen di Pazzi. With flaming red neckties flying in the wind and shouting slogans of anarchism, a band of twenty or more men attacked the procession as it passed Eighth and Christian Streets. The leader of the gang brandished a .38-caliber revolver, and it was the prompt action of the police on the scene that resulted in seizing the ringleaders. "It is believed that Rev. Antonio Isoleri, rector of the Church of St. Mary Magdalen di Piazzi, was saved from assassination."[312]

Ten plainclothes police officers were marching in the procession surrounding Father Isoleri, so obviously there was some advance warning about the anarchists' goal. But when the attack came, "hundreds of little girls, robed in white, who took part in the procession, fled…in terror."[313]

The attackers shouted:

> *"Down with the priests!*
> *No more clowns!*
> *Down with the superstitions!"*[314]

C.C.A. was quoted as saying the May Day Procession might have to be discontinued due to an "undercurrent of opposition" in the Italian quarter.[315]

As Mussolini was coming to power in Italy, the Socialist contingent in Philadelphia began to act out. In October 1921, C.C.A. chaired a mass meeting to hear an appeal for funds for disabled Italian soldiers. The speaker was the youngest member of the Chamber of Deputies and a Nationalist Party member, war hero captain Giuseppi Bottai.[316] The crowd was in the Alhambra Theater at Twelfth and Morris Streets. At least thirty-one hecklers were arrested for preventing the Italian consul from being heard with their cries of "Don't let him speak."[317] He was trying to introduce the captain while being heckled when thirty men and one woman were arrested and removed with the charge of inciting a riot.[318]

The article said C.C.A. Baldi, as chairman of the committee, "declared that the disturbances were due to the strife between the Socialist and Nationalist" Parties in Italy.[319] The first man who was arrested was distributing anarchist literature.[320]

The anarchists were very likely behind the 1922 burning of one of C.C.A.'s automobiles at 1216 Washington Avenue. It was a total loss.[321] Two years later, another car parked at the same location was torched but was not a total loss.[322]

A major attempt to assassinate C.C.A. came a few minutes before midnight on April 20, 1923, when a time bomb on the front steps of his home in Roxborough was detonated.[323]

A woman directly across the street from the bombing died on April 21, the day after the bombing. Mrs. Charles Groat of 4454 Dexter Street had been ill at home when she was showered with glass in her bedroom, and the shock of it all apparently caused her death.[324]

A press report speculated that a planned welcome home reception at the house was the aim of the plotters, but C.C.A. was delayed leaving Italy on a trip with Joseph F.M. Baldi, II.[325] The police believed the bomb was loaded with TNT. The damage to the home was estimated at $40,000.[326] Louise Baldi and sons Vito and Virgil were "thrown from their beds by the

A car owned by C.C.A. *Author's collection.*

force of the explosion."[327] Two men seen running from the scene were sought by the police.[328] The police suspected the bomb was the work of "anti-fascisti elements."[329]

C.C.A. was a big fan of Il Duce, and "one of his present delights is to decorate his…friends with the 'black shirt' button, a goodly

Public Ledger
April 21, 1923   pp. 1 & 6.

BOMB DAMAGES SUBURBAN HOME OF C. C. A. BALDI

Tears Away Steps, Sidewalk and Retaining Wall at Roxborough

WIFE AND TWO SONS HOME, BUT NOT INJURED BY BLAST

Party in Neighbourhood Broken Up by Crashing of Window Glass

MOTORISTS NOTICED BOX

Italian Merchant-Banker-Editor Known on Both Sides of the Atlantic

A time bomb in front of the home of Chevalier C. C. A. Baldi, at Green lane and Dexter street, Roxborough, exploded at a few minutes before 12 o'clock last night, doing extensive damage to the house, threatening the lives of Mr. Baldi's wife and two sons, shattering windows in a wide area and arousing interest in the whole northern section of the city, where the intonation was heard.

So great was the force of the explosion that a big hole was torn in the front lawn, the steps and walk on which the bomb lay were torn up and the eight-foot wall, which holds up the terrace on which the house itself stands, was thrown down.

At the Baldi house itself the large double doors at the front were torn from their hinges and flung into the hall, carrying part of the uprights with them. Every window in the house was broken. Pictures were torn from the wall, chinaware broken, the gas-fittings of the house jarred loose, and plaster broken from many walls.

Mrs. Baldi was asleep in an upper room. Her sons, Vito and Virgil, were in the rear of the first floor.

None of them was injured, although Mrs. Baldi suffered severely from the shock.

Baldi's sons stated last night after the explosion that they knew of no reason why any one should attempt to harm or terrorise the family.

Gay Party Thrown in Confusion.

At the home of Joseph Sobernheimer, wool merchant, 346 Green lane, some distance from the Baldi home, a party was being given for the son of the family. The blast shattered the windows as the guests were sitting down for a midnight supper. Pictures were flung from the walls and plaster from the ceiling

Public Ledger
April 21, 1923   pp. 1 & 6.

and the whole merry company was thrown into confusion, no one being able to account for the explosion at the moment.

A party of motorists narrowly escaped injury. Their car passed the house a few moments before the explosion, the members of the party having noticed a peculiar large box, placed on the top step of the stone stairway leading to the Baldi house. The house extends fifty feet back from Green lane and about eighteen feet from Dexter street.

"It looked like a big hat box," members of this motor party told the police afterwards.

Their care drove on after its occupants had looked curiously at the box, but had gone only a block and a half when the automobile was almost overturned by the explosion.

Windows Broken in Neighbourhood.

Seventy-five feet east of the Baldi home is the residence of Frederick A. Sobernheimer, a lawyer, of 323 Green lane. Mr. Sobernheimer is a brother-in-law of Mr. Baldi.

Every window on the front and side of the Sobernheimer home was shattered. At the front of the house a storm door was split and partly torn from its fastenings. A plate-glass porch light was jerked partly loose and the glass broken.

Adjoining the Sobernheimer home to the east is the house of John S. Sneyd, assistant secretary of the Philadelphia and Reading Railway.[1] Mr. Sneyd said the explosion nearly threw him from his bed. The windows of his room, and many others of those in the house, were smashed, carrying part of the sills with them.

At the other side of the Baldi residence is the home of Erwin Simpson, at Manayunk avenue and Green lane.[2] Windows in all parts of the house were broken.

The home of Samuel Kenworthy, a prominent manufacturer, is across the street.[3] This house partly protects that of Joseph Kenworthy, in which the party was in progress.

Across the street from the Baldi home much damage was done to thirty residences standing on Dexter street. Every window on the side facing the Baldi residence was shattered.

At the home of C. J. Mauer, of 350 [sic] Green lane, many windows were broken.[4] Mr. Mauer is a dealer in dynamite and powder.

Other homes damaged included those of John F. L. Marris [sic], of 342 Green lane; Charles Broat, of 4454 Dexter street, where the porch was loosened from the house, and that of George G. McMaster, at No. 4452.

Above: From Public Ledger, *April 21, 1923.*

Right: Bombing of Green Lane. From Vancouver Daily World, *May 4, 1923.*

ANTI-FASCISTI LEADERS BOMB PHILADELPHIA HOME

supply of which he brought back from Italy after his recent visit to his old home."[330] The black shirts were the paramilitary forces of Mussolini, called the Squadrismo. Also, at the time a group of Sicilians and Italians based in Chicago called the Black Hand extorted money by sending letters with a black hand symbol seeking payment from businesses. This evolved into the Mafia in the 1920s.

Just three weeks after the bombing of C.C.A.'s home, an explosion wrecked the lower floor of the M. Maggio Grocery Store at Ninth and Montrose Streets in South Philadelphia. This bomb was attributed by the police as the work of the Black Hand gang, whose leader had just been sentenced to four years in prison by the federal court.[331] Two men suspected of that bombing were Giuseppe Giorgesti and Salvatro Sabelia. The police surmised the two bombings might have been an effort to induce wealthy Italians to use their influence to get gang members out of prison.[332]

In November 1923, the Spanish and Italian consulates in Philadelphia were bombed, and the director of public safety saw "a connection with the bombing of the home of Chevalier C.C.A. Baldi in Roxborough."[333] Andrew Emmanuel, chief of the bomb squad, said the methods in all three attacks were identical.[334] The U.S. Department of Justice sent experts from Washington who were following international Communist activities because Reds were believed to have been involved.[335]

C.C.A. was to have returned to New York in April from Italy and was going to spend the night there at the McAlpin Hotel after getting off his ship. He was to continue on to Philadelphia the next day. The plotters planned to set a bomb outside his hotel room. Months later, on November 24, 1923, three men were arrested as suspects in the two consulate bombings.[336]

Four years later in Pittsburgh, six men were arrested when one thousand people gathered to parade new banners for the Sons of Italy Lodge No. 901, named after King Victor Emmanuel, II.

Bomb Suspects

LOUIS DIAZ
JOSE VINNES
VICENZO DI PALMO

Bomb suspects arrested. *From* Philadelphia Inquirer, *November 25, 1923.*

> *The parade, which assembled at the Larimer Avenue bridge, was marching to the East End Theater, Collins Avenue, to dedicate its lodge flags and banner when men along the line of march added sticks and stones to a barrage of verbal insults and fists were brought into play. The parade was stopped for more than 15 minutes while police restored order.*[337]

Speaking at the East End Theater in Pittsburgh were Cavalier (and later judge) Eugene V. Alessandroni, as well as Grand Venerable Giovanni Di Silvestro, the Italian vice consul of Pittsburgh, and C.C.A. Baldi as president of the Italian Societies Federation of Philadelphia.[338]

The Red/Fascist conflict continued after C.C.A. died in 1930 with the bombing of Giovanni Di

Front view of 319 Green Lane. *Courtesy of Celeste Morello.*

Silvestro's home, killing the wife of the leader of the Order of the Sons of Italy in late January 1933.[339]

As for the house at Green Lane, in 2017, noted Philadelphia historian and author Celeste A. Morello submitted the property for nomination to the National Register of Historic Places of the Philadelphia Historical Commission. It was approved and is now in the register.

Louise Sobernheimer Baldi and son Vito on the steps of Green Lane, where the bomb was placed. *Author's collection.*

10 NEWS

METRO.US
WEEKEND, JULY 20-23, 2017

Taylor Swift's great-grandpa's Philly home gets recognition

Home of Italian businessman who helped shape Philly gets historic designation.

A.D. AMOROSI
@MetroPhilly
letters@metro.us

In his time, Charles Carmine Antonio Baldi — C.C.A. Baldi — was a first-generation Italian immigrant entrepreneur and community leader of great renown.

Arriving in Philadelphia from Cilento di Castelnuovo, Salerno, in

1876, C.C.A. (who later brought three brothers and one sister — Ferdinando, Virgilio, Alfonso and Grazia — to South Philly) founded his own coal yard (with its own mine in Schuylkill County), opened an insurance and real estate business, organized

the initial nomination or the addition of the local funeral icon's 319 Green St. home (built in 1891, currently a multi-unit property) to the Historic Registry. "I had no idea Swift had any connection to Charles Baldi until Vic Baldi told me, so she was

Pop idol Taylor Swift's Italian great-grandfather C.C.A. Baldi's Philly home in Manayunk just got a historic designation. GETTY IMAGES/PROVIDED

Taylor Swift's great-great-grandfather's home recognized as historic. *From* Metro, *July 19, 2017.*

Judge Robert O. Baldi of the Bucks County Court of Common Pleas submitted a letter of support for the historic accreditation on March 13, 2017. He is the son of Joseph F.M. Baldi, II, and grandson of C.C.A. Said the judge:

> *C.C.A. Baldi had a daughter named Louise after her mother Louise (my grandmother). When I was a young man, I was told that when C.C.A. Baldi came home he would bellow out the name "Louise" calling for his family to greet him, and both his wife, his daughter and a dog named Louisa would all come running at his command. I was brought up hearing stories that suggested that it was a very happy home for the Baldi Family.*

After the house was designated as historic the press connected the dots between C.C.A. and pop star Taylor Swift, his great-great-granddaughter.

WASHINGTON'S CROSSING AND IDLAB FARM

December 1776 was cold and snowy, and General George Washington's troops badly needed a victory after their defeats. The British were holed up in Philadelphia and New York but had 1,500 Hessian mercenary troops in Trenton, New Jersey, not far from Newtown, Pennsylvania, across the Delaware River. Newtown was farm country in Bucks County, where several farmhouses were hosting Washington's high command. The five houses around Jericho Mountain were just a couple of miles from the future Delaware River crossing area.

In the Samuel Merrick House, headquarters of General Nathanael Greene, the generals met to plan a surprise attack on Trenton for Christmas Day.

The 1723 stone house—later owned by C.C.A.—has a plaque bearing the title "The House of Decision" from the Daughters of the American Revolution because on Christmas Eve 1776, the Samuel Merrick House in Pineville (now 1187 Eagle Road in Newtown, Upper Makefield Township, Bucks County) was the site of General Washington's final council of war on the evening before the Christmas Day crossing of the Delaware.

Washington dined that night with General Greene, General John Sullivan and others. Only Merrick's young daughter Hannah was allowed to stay so she could serve the generals their dinner. With maps before them, the "crossing" that changed the Revolution from defeat to victory was laid out for a final run-through.

Five Revolutionary headquarters. No. 4 is the Samuel Merrick House. *From a public handout at the park.*

One member of Greene's staff who stayed with the general at the Merrick House was none other than Thomas Paine, the author of *Common Sense*. In another piece, Paine wrote the famous words, "These are the times that try men's souls" as an effort to rally the faltering cause for freedom.

The Hessian brigade was commanded by a Colonel Rall, a brave, hard-drinking soldier who spoke almost no English. The officer and many of his troops spent most of Christmas Day celebrating with the bottle and were feeling no pain by nightfall.

At about that time, General Washington's two thousand troops—marching slightly inland from the river so their movements would not be detected by enemy lookouts—arrived at a ferry landing. There they boarded cargo boats shaped somewhat like large canoes that were propelled across the river by a contingent of sailors from Marblehead, Massachusetts, pushing with oars and poles. The day was cold and windy, and rain mixed with snow and sleet was falling. The boats had to be maneuvered through blocks of ice, but the men finally reached the New Jersey shore.

Colonel Rall and many of his men were not even awake when the Americans attacked the village at about 8:00 a.m. Despite the sharp noises of cannons and muskets, the Hessian officer could hardly be aroused by an orderly. By the time he reached the street, it was too late. The American guns dominated the town, making it impossible for the Hessians to organize and launch an effective counterattack. Rebel riflemen—long scorned by the king's forces as undisciplined and ineffective—maintained a steady and deadly fire, and the panic-stricken Hessians retreated.

After about forty-five minutes of fighting, all resistance collapsed. Underneath the white flag, 900 Hessian soldiers laid down their arms. They had suffered about 30 deaths, including Colonel Rall. There were only five American casualties. It was Washington's first victory of the war, and it came in the nick of time. Militarily, the battle revived the flagging American will to fight the war to a new successful end and paid off immediately in a flood of new and extended enlistments.

Because of the importance of the battle, the Pennsylvania legislature in 1917 established the Washington Crossing Park Commission, which continued in existence until 1998. The commission was initially solely responsible for the creation, planning and implementing of the park plan. The first commission's founding members were Martin Brumbaugh, president, Harrisburg; J. Edward Moon, Morrisville; Harman Yerkes, Doylestown; Samuel Eastburn, Langhorne; Heyward Myers, St. Davids; Allen Hagenback, Allentown; C.C.A. Baldi, Philadelphia; Charles Schwab, Bethlehem; Penrose Robinson, Hatboro; J. Anderson Ross, Philadelphia; and J. Armstrong Herman, Harrisburg. All were prominent members of the larger regional community, but most did not live in the Washington Crossing area. They met regularly in Philadelphia and then in the park at different locations, including the McConkey Ferry Inn, the Mahlon Taylor House and even the lawn next to the Ferry Inn. Their minutes survive to this day, stored in the Pennsylvania State Archives in Harrisburg.

A reenactment of Washington crossing the Delaware River in December 1776. *Photo by Wayne Henderek, by permission.*

Top: 1917 Park Commission letterhead. *Author's collection.*

Bottom: Photo of the house from the road. *Author's photo.*

Some of those founding members stand out. Harman Yerkes was a judge who would serve as its president for many years; Clarence Buckman was a state senator; Samuel Eastburn had been involved since the first official group was formed in 1913. He had been studying the crossing for years and its impact on the region. Edward Moon had made the first contacts with New Jersey officials as the park was being created. Charles Schwab was the first president of the Bethlehem Steel Corporation and the chairman of its board of directors.

The treasurer was C.C.A. Baldi of Philadelphia. Ten years after the commission was created, C.C.A. would own the famous House of Decision.

The park officially opened on October 1, 1921. Since 1961, it has been designated as a National Historic Landmark by the United States government, but it is not a national park.

The Merrick House and farm was purchased by C.C.A.'s son Vito Baldi (a single man) on August 12, 1925, containing the main parcel of 48.25 acres with the buildings thereon. Vito in turn conveyed it to Charles C.A. Baldi Company, Inc., on December 28, 1927. On June 15, 1928, Ralph Vasaturo of Philadelphia conveyed an additional 19.75 acres of adjoining woodland to the company. On April 30, 1931 (after C.C.A. died in December 1930), both parcels were conveyed to Edith M. Baldi, wife of C.C.A.'s son Frederick S. Baldi. Because he was a prison warden and could be sued by inmates, Fred told my father he wanted to protect the farm from attachment, so it was in Edith's name. An additional 23.3 acres of land was also conveyed in 1931. The location is just a handful of farms away from the state park on the west side of the Delaware.

The property went on the market for sale with just six acres for over $1 million in 2020.

When the Baldis owned it, the name of the place was Idlab Farm, or Baldi spelled backward.

CHAPTER 19

DEATH OF C.C.A. BALDI

The night before his death on December 28, 1930, C.C.A. had attended a holiday party at the First Italian Exchange Bank at 928 South Eighth Street.[340] His health had only recently declined. The death certificate attested to by Alfonso Baldi gave the cause of death as cerebral apoplexy, with myocarditis as a secondary cause (see appendix). Since 1924, after his wife, Louisa, died, C.C.A. had lived in an apartment over the bank. His female friend was then a woman named "Zippy" Cozza, who was the estranged wife of an employee of one of the Baldi enterprises.[341]

C.C.A.'s bank porter, Tony Laporta, found him dead in bed when he came with the Sunday papers on the morning of December 28.[342] Laporta notified Baldi's oldest son, Dr. Frederick M. Baldi, who determined that his father had died of an apoplectic stroke many hours prior.[343]

Thousands lined the streets of South Philadelphia with heads bared in silent tribute as funeral services were held on Saturday, January 3, 1931.[344] The *Suburban Press* newspaper provided great detail of the services:

> *From 10 a.m. Friday, until sometime on Saturday, the body of the Italian American leader was on view in the offices of* L'Opinione, *the Italian daily newspaper which he owned. During that time more than 15,000, among them many of the city's leaders, filed past the bier and crowded around the establishment at 1018 South Eighth Street to pay their last respects to a man who had been the holder of three decorations from the King of Italy.*

Shortly after 10 o'clock, the cortege began the block-and-a-half procession to the Church of Our Lady of Good Counsel on Christian Street, between Eighth and Ninth Streets.

While the funeral procession proper was small, in accordance with Mr. Baldi's wishes for a simple funeral, members of about 150 societies of the Italian Federation fell in behind, with flags and banners waving from the shoulders of many whose benefactor Mr. Baldi had been.[345]

Fifty policemen under Captain Frank Dunn were on duty to take care of the throngs, while eleven men of the motor highway patrol were on hand to escort the cortege to a local cemetery, where interment was private.

At the church, difficulty was experienced by those who were unable to gain entrance, and squads of Boy Scouts and schoolchildren lined up on the church sidewalk to aid the police.[346]

Monsignor Eugene Murphy, rector of St. John the Baptist Church, Manayunk, presided at the solemn requiem mass. The celebrant was the Reverend Aurelio Marini, OSA, rector of the church. The Reverend Lorenzo Andolfio, OSA, rector of St. Nicholas of Tolentine's Church, was deacon, and the Reverend Bartholomew Pizzuto, OSA, was master of ceremonies.[347]

One of the displays of respect shown by residents of the neighborhood was the temporary suspension of business while the funeral was underway. Many stores, restaurants and shops had signs posted: "This place closed between 10 and 12 o'clock on account of the funeral of C.C.A. Baldi."[348]

Judges Harry S. McDevitt and Eugene V. Alessandroni, District Attorney John Monaghan, Mayor Harry A. Mackey, Chief Patrick McKewen of county detectives and members of the board of education were among those who paid their respects.

In the office of *L'Opinione* was a box about four feet high containing telegrams from all parts of the state and nation and some from abroad. Among these was an expression of regret from Premier Mussolini of Italy, who was a personal friend of Mr. Baldi.[349]

C.C.A. had gone back to his childhood Catholic faith after decades of attending Presbyterian churches. However, his family, children and grandchildren were all raised as Presbyterians. C.C.A. was buried in Westminster Cemetery in Bala Cynwyd in a marble-lined crypt that has room for sixteen remains. C.C.A. paid $10,000 to have the vault and crypts constructed near the Roxborough section, where his home was located. The August 13, 1920 contract was between C.C.A. and Alexander R. Alessi of Darby, Pennsylvania. The marble was Italian Vermont marble, but the tomb

The Baldi crypt in Bala Cynwyd. *Robert Baldi photo.*

was to be Barre granite with a base of five by ten feet. The cap, or top piece, pictured was six by three and a half feet in size. The Baldi name is carved into it. The result is an underground mausoleum.

Bucks County Court of Common Pleas judge Robert O. Baldi is a son of Joseph F.M. Baldi, II, a son of C.C.A. He relates that in 1920, the idea for a crypt came about because of the death of Rose Baldi, who died young at twenty-eight of a round of Spanish flu on February 8, 1920, and is the first Baldi buried there. According to Judge Baldi, he has seen papers approving a delay of her interment while the tomb was being built. C.C.A.'s daughter Louise named her second daughter Rose B. Douglas (Swift) after her.

In a March 13, 2017, letter regarding the nomination of 319 Green Lane to the Philadelphia Historical Commission, Judge Baldi summed up conversations he had with his father:

> *Years after my father died, while visiting the family cemetery plot, it occurred to me that the location was probably carefully considered by C.C.A. Baldi at the time the mausoleum was constructed. I was told he designed the mausoleum to be underground so that later generations would not have to take care of it. From the stories that have been told to me by my father, his*

*brothers, and my Aunt Louise, C.C.A. Baldi was a dynamic energetic man
whose decisions were well thought out. I have no doubt that the landscape
of both Manayunk and the trees on the hill near the cemetery plot were
quite different when the burial site was constructed. I suspect that while he
was alive he could look up towards the hill and have a clear line of sight to
where his daughter was buried and he knew there would be a time when he
would be able to look back to the family house on Green Lane when he too
was buried in the family plot.*

Buried in lot 296 are the following, as of 2021:

1. Baldi, Virgil B. (ashes)
2.
3. Baldi, Charles C.A., III
4.
5.
6.
7. Baldi, Charles C.A., Jr.
8. Baldi, Vito M.
9. Baldi, Louise E.
10. Baldi, Rose
11. Baldi, Charles C.A.
12. Baldi, Lucetta B.
13.
14. Baldi, Caroline
15.
16. Baldi, Joseph B.

C.C.A.'s will of three pages was signed one day before he died.[350]
"According to some of his friends, he carried life insurance totaling
approximately $2,000,000."[351] In 1963, I reviewed the will and estate papers
at city hall in the Records Department (will book no. 552, p. 209). Other
papers are in the Orphans Court records of 1931 (book no. 4, p. 306). His
estate inventory was over $800,000.

According to a 1931 newspaper report, the will read in relevant part:

*I give and bequeath all the furniture, carpets, pictures, rugs, and contents
in my residence, 319 Green Lane, Roxborough, to my two children, Joseph
F. M. Baldi and Mrs. Louise E. Baldi Douglass, to share and share alike.*

Robert and Joseph F.M. Baldi, II, in the crypt in 2014. *Robert Baldi photo.*

> *I bequeath the sum of $5,000 to my said daughter, Louise E. Baldi Douglass, to be paid to her by my executors hereinafter named, as follows: The sum of $1,000 to be paid to her at the expiration of one year from the date of my death, and an additional sum of $1,000 every year thereafter, until the full sum of $5,000 is paid to her. Should she die before the full sum is paid to her, the balance still due shall be used for the maintenance, education, and support of the children she shall leave surviving.*[352]

All the "residue and remainder went to the sons equally."[353] Of the business assets, only the funeral home survived the Depression.

CHAPTER 20

FIRST GENERATION
OF AMERICANS

FREDERICK S. BALDI

With a German grandmother and an Italian father, the firstborn of C.C.A. was Frederick Sobernheimer Baldi, who grew up at 319 Green Lane in Roxborough. Much more is known about him because after his career in prison medicine and administration, he wrote the book *My Unwelcome Guests*, published by Lippincott Publishing in 1959.

Fred was born on October 14, 1886, in Philadelphia and graduated from Central High School in 1905.[354] The graduation dance was chaired by Fred Baldi.[355] His cousin Frederick T. Sobernheimer, Jr., and Harry S. McDevitt were two of the ten serving on the dance committee. McDevitt became a lawyer and later a judge who was always a close friend of the Baldi boys.

While his first job was shoveling coal for the family coal company,[356] Fred went on to graduate from the University of Pennsylvania Medical School on June 15, 1910.[357] But prior to that, his father had insisted Fred go to law school, so he first entered the University of Pennsylvania School of Law in the class of 1908.[358] The course he loved was criminal law, but when he told his father he wanted to be a criminal defense lawyer, C.C.A. shouted, "Never!" C.C.A. then said, "Anything but that! I would rather see you as a poor doctor than as a criminal lawyer. Go and study medicine."[359] That was what Fred had wanted to do all along anyway.

Fred married the widow of a famous University of Pennsylvania football player who had been killed in Mexico in 1905.[360] Sarah Benson Rutherfod

Above: Fred Baldi and his only child, Charles Carmen Baldi, known as Chuck, and my father Charles G. Douglas, Jr. (*holding a hat*). *Author's collection.*

Right: A young Charles Baldi. *Author's collection.*

and Fred were married on June 8, 1910, and resided in Collingdale, Pennsylvania.[361] Later, he married Edith M. Cooper, his second wife. His son, Chuck, married Mary Lou Baldi, and they had two children, Frederick Winfield Baldi and Debra Baldi Matz. Young Fred became a restorer of historic homes and Debra an accomplished horsewoman.[362]

On July 22, 1910, Fred was one of 306 to pass exams and become a licensed physician. Private practice was difficult, as some hospitals did not want Italians on their medical staff. In 1914, a desperate county took Fred on as an assistant physician, but he left that position to serve from 1917 to 1919 as a captain in the Naval Medical Service with the Northern Bomber Group of the U.S. Marine Aviation Forces. In 1934, he applied for twenty months of compensation under a program set up by the Commonwealth of Pennsylvania and listed 319 Green Lane as his address.[363]

In 1913, tragedy struck Dr. Baldi and his then wife, Sarah, when an eighteen-year-old boy was hit and killed by an automobile while bicycling in New Jersey. Fred Baldi claimed it was a hit-and-run by another car, and not him, but that he stopped to assist the boy as a physician. The "phantom car" became an issue, so the Burlington, New Jersey coroner convened a jury to determine the cause of the boy's death on the Burlington-Columbus Expressway. The jury found no criminal negligence on Fred's part but stated that it was an unavoidable accident when he ran over the boy.[364]

Fred Baldi became medical director for the Philadelphia County prisons in 1930 and added to that title when he also was appointed superintendent of prisons.[365] The downtown prison, Moyamensing, was built in 1835 and was for short-term prisoners, while newer Holmesburg was the maximum-security prison. In his forty years of penology, Fred Baldi said he had the custody and medical care of 750,000 men and women.[366] After he resigned in 1953, Dr. Baldi went on to be a warden of the Rockview State Penitentiary.[367] At Rockview, the doctor oversaw all electric chair executions, which was not a problem for him as a fervent supporter of the death penalty.

A major point of irritation was the escape of notorious inmate Slick Willie Sutton from Holmesburg Penitentiary in 1947. It was the only successful escape in that prison's fifty-three-year history. Fred always assumed bribed guards were involved.[368]

Idlab Farm came to Fred by deed from his brother Vito on April 30, 1931. It was put in the name of Edith M. Baldi because Fred was concerned about losing it if he was sued by inmates at the prison.

Dr. Baldi was a Republican, but he never played the political game the way his father had. For instance, in 1955, when the governorship changed parties, Fred received a letter to contribute $100 toward the Democratic Party if he wanted to remain in his position.[369] He recalled in his book:

> *Some of the key men in the place were in my office at the time, and I told them of the letter's contents. They were a worried lot as I called the Commissioner on the telephone and told him what he and Harrisburg could do with my job, if that was the way things were to be.*
>
> *I kept my job, for a satisfactory time thereafter, and throughout the balance of my stay at Rockview, to the best of my knowledge, the men under me there were free from political harassment. Otherwise, as I have since learned, they would have been subjected to compulsory assessments— the Pennsylvania term for it is "macing"—which the party generously permits contributors to pay on the installment plan if their pay is too small to meet the demand at a single time.*[370]

His reasons for resisting were stated in his book as follows:

> *I have never found it difficult to refuse requests for this kind of slush money, and always advised my men to ignore any such demands. Not only are prison officials and those under them asked to do a tough job for much less pay than the job is worth; the top officials, at least, bring to their jobs professional training and reputation. They are not, and should not be, beholden to any politician for tenure.*[371]

A Riotous Welcome

Fred's 1932 promotion to superintendent of prisons for Philadelphia was met by a riot, which was a tradition for a new superintendent to see how he would react and set the tone for his tenure.[372] Dr. Baldi always recognized that good food and its preparation was key to a quiet prison. When he came to Holmesburg, the cooks were doing a terrible job, so he fired the civilian cook and "threw out the whole kitchen crew of around eighty men." They were white, and he said he "replaced them with Negroes. That did not go over well."[373]

Fred Baldi described that riot

> *as distinctive as a swarming of bees. It begins as simple, vindictive hell-raising, but it builds. I got to Holmesburg in a hurry to find four corridors*

rioting that meant about 700 men—half the population tearing up their furniture, tables, stools, shelves, and throwing the pieces into the corridors. Along with steel gates, some cells had solid wooden doors. These were pried loose and added to the firewood. Now the prisoners tore up their mattresses, shoving pieces through the food wicket—the little doorway through which meals are passed. Then the rioters set fire to this litter. If you have had the bad luck to set fire to a mattress, you know the quality of smoke this produces. Other chunks of mattress were stuffed down the toilets.[374]

Rather than call on outside police, the doctor chose eight calm but big guards to accompany him in putting down the riot.

By now we were a combined assault force and rescue expedition. The fires were going so well in some areas that prisoners were bawling to be saved and threatening to kill us if we came in to save them. To the eight-man detachment I gave this prescription:

First, no rough stuff. It is a losing game to blackjack one man and infuriate ten. I was determined to stop this nonsense without bloodshed.

Second, no police were to be let in. If you can't control rioters with your own personnel, and must bring in outside forces, then it is far better to bring in state troopers. Three or four state troopers can control prison disorder more quickly than fifty bluecoats. Prisoners hate policemen, but have little reason to hate state troopers. The sight of a police uniform is the best fuel you can pour on a riot.

Third, we would proceed to put out the fires and quiet the men. The treatment would be the same for both: water. I rolled my pants above my knees and picked up the fire hose. That is, I picked it up on the second try. I still remember my naive surprise at the weight. I had never handled a fire hose and supposed it would weigh no more than a garden hose.

We didn't have much pressure. That was later rectified—for in a prison riot, a fire hose is the Queen of Battle. No other weapon compares. You can bowl hysterical men off their feet, you can wash them into corners, all without harming them. No man can stand up to a fire hose.

Without pressure, we couldn't do much quelling. But when we got the fires under control, we could cool the men off, and that is literally what we did. Where two or three furious men stood in a cell brandishing weapons, we poured water on them until it stood six inches deep on the floor. They did a lot of yelling. But the fact is, on that sweltering August day it must have felt pretty good.

In two hours the riot was over, without outside help.[375]

With the riot over, the inmates locked in their cells in standing water yelled out:

"What'll we do with all this water?"

"Bail it out," I said. "Flush out those toilets you fouled up. And get going. If it isn't done in two hours, I'll give you that and much more."

I got support of a sort. One of my loyal subjects spoke with great clarity. "Why, that bald-headed son of a bitch!" he said. "He means it."

"Where are we going to sleep?" someone else yelled.

"You burned up your mattresses," I said, "so you can sleep on the beds." The beds didn't boast springs, only a latticework of strap steel. Trying to go to sleep on that lacework would give a man plenty of time to think.

We tossed fourteen ringleaders into punishment cells and let the rest spend the night in their wrecked cells. Next morning I made them clean up the mess in the corridors. In some prisons, after a riot, outsiders do the cleaning. Not in mine. The man who tears anything up in prison gets to pick up every scrap of it. When they had worked up a good appetite, they got lunch—all the lunch they could drink from their water taps.[376]

The prison yard on the right and Dr. Baldi. *Cover photo from Dr. Baldi's book* My Unwelcome Guests *(1959).*

The men did not get fed until they cleaned everything up. The conclusion: "There were no more riots during my administration."[377]

When I was eleven years old, I had a tour of Holmesburg with Uncle Fred. I remember how big and imposing he was, with hands the size of oven mitts. But everywhere we went, it was a very respectful "Good morning, Dr. Baldi" or "Hi, Dr. Baldi."

Two days in standing water earns you respect from prison inmates that lasts for many years.

Vito M. Baldi

The second son of C.C.A. was born in Philadelphia on March 7, 1888. He was named after C.C.A.'s father, Vito, who died in 1918. Young Vito was a graduate of Central High School and D.H.E. Dolan College. He became a licensed funeral director in 1919 but was also involved in the family real estate business. In 1912, the family visited Europe; the photo shown on page 138 was taken on March 7, 1912, after sailing to Italy on January 6.

In 1918, Vito was indicted for vote stealing, which the liberal Italian press enjoyed: "When Vito M. Baldi, for example, the politically active son of the Republican leader, was indicted in 1918 for the not uncommon Philadelphia practice of vote-stealing, the Italian press gleefully excoriated the younger Baldi. *La Libera Parola* described Vito Baldi as 'the arch, the master conspirator,' a manipulator of his fellow countrymen."[378]

For ten years, he was the editor of *L'Opinione*. On October 29, 1928, a few days before the presidential election, Vito committed a sin for which he was removed from the paper and from C.C.A.'s will: he endorsed Democratic candidate Al Smith.

Vito Baldi for Smith

Italian Editor Announces Stand at Democratic Rally

Vito Baldi, editor of L'Opinione, *an Italian language newspaper published in this city, announced himself as a supporter of Alfred E. Smith for President yesterday.*

Mr. Baldi made his declaration in favor of the democratic candidate at a meeting of nearly 1000 Italian political workers held yesterday afternoon in the headquarters of the Democratic Campaign Committee Broadstreet and South Penn Square, Michael Spatola presided at the meeting.

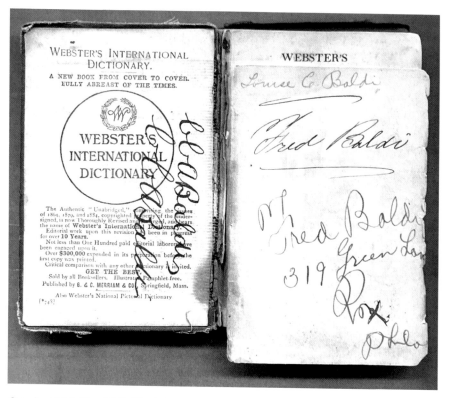

Opposite, top left: Vito M. Baldi. *Author's collection.*

Opposite, top right: Vito Baldi at Green Lane. *Author's collection.*

Opposite, bottom: Vito M. Baldi at Louise's home in Roxborough, 1973. *Author's collection.*

Above: C.C.A.'s dictionary. *Author's collection.*

Vito M. Baldi was the brother my grandmother Louise was closest to, and he was the possessor of an 1870 Webster's Dictionary that C.C.A. used to help learn English after he immigrated to America. He maintained the Baldi Funeral Home.

He married Lucetta Belji of Philadelphia and was described as a member of national, state and county funeral directors' associations; Order Sons of Italy; and Italian Federation. Active in civic and charitable affairs, he was fond of travel, art, music and sports of all kinds.[379]

CHARLES CARMEN ANTONIO BALDI, JR.

My uncle Carmen was the third child of C.C.A. and was born in Philadelphia in Manayunk on December 16, 1890. He graduated from Central High School as president of his class of 236 students.[380] He then went to the Wharton School at the University of Pennsylvania and the law school. In law school, he was a member of Gamma Delta fraternity and the Music Club, and he boxed and wrestled there.[381]

When he was just twenty-one, he was elected to the Philadelphia City Council and served from 1911 to 1916.

The year 1916 was one of scandal for Carmen. In July, seventy-five prospective lawyers took the bar exam in Pittsburgh. Only one was from Philadelphia, and according to the newspaper there, his name was Charles Baldi, Jr.[382] In fact, posing as Carmen was a Philadelphia attorney named Edwin K. Adams, who took the exam for Carmen but flunked it.[383] Disbarment proceedings were begun for Adams.[384] It turns out that Adams previously went to Pittsburgh in December 1915 posing as Baldi but flunked that exam as well.

Both men admitted to the scheme, and the Board of Bar Examiners said Carmen Baldi "will never be allowed to take the State examinations."[385] During the investigation into the cheating scandal, it was learned that Carmen was not alone in the effort; he and others were aided by a syndicate of "unscrupulous men"[386] who were paid $500 to $1,000 by law graduates to "guarantee that a candidate would pass."[387] A few months later, the state Supreme Court issued a formal order that Carmen and five other men were never to take the bar exam again.[388]

As for his political future, it was only briefly interrupted by the scandal after he resigned in October 1916 from the city council.[389] A month later, he got 90 percent of the vote when he ran for the Pennsylvania House of Representatives against Democrat Frank Malone, beating him 3,041 to 304, in the Second Legislative District.[390] He served eight more consecutive terms in Harrisburg until 1937. For three terms, he was chairman of the Banks and Banking Committee. While he had worked as a cashier at the family's Italian Exchange Bank in 1917, he moved over to the coal company and became its manager in 1920.[391]

In 1917, Carmen married Gladys B. McCarthy of Philadelphia, and they had two children.[392] In September 1919, young son Antonio (C.C.A. Baldi, III) died. Whether his death was due to the deadly Spanish flu is unknown. On January 7, 1919, Nancy Payntor Baldi was born, and she later married George H. Berlin, Jr., and lived in Media.[393] The family was Presbyterian, and

Left: Carmen Baldi at Green Lane. *Right*: Carmen Baldi, July 2, 1927. *Author's collection.*

when C.C.A., Jr., died on February 5, 1962, after an automobile accident, he lived at 1341 Ellsworth Street in South Philadelphia. He was buried in the Baldi crypt in Westminster Cemetery along with his son.

His legislative record was progressive. In 1919, he was one of seven to oppose a bill prohibiting the teaching of German in the public schools, but it passed the House 180 to 7.[394] He voted to allow women the vote, which passed the House 128 to 66.[395] Carmen also voted against the prohibition of alcohol in 1919. He loved to ride horses, but his bill to legalize horse race betting was killed in 1927 (119 to 50) after fierce opposition:

> *Carrying his battle to the last line of defense with high hopes of bringing back the "sport of kings" to Pennsylvania, Mr. Baldi found his forte too poorly fortified for the conflict. It was a one-sided battle with churches, colleges and patriotic organizations allied against the bill, these bodies fighting bitterly to uphold the "morals" of the state and blot out such a "debasing thing."*[396]

Helping to fund the "yes" votes was James H. Irwin, a South Philadelphia horse stable owner and "Vare henchman."[397]

A year later, in 1928, Carmen's brother Joe was elected to join him in the legislature as the South Philadelphia Italians evolved from one to three seats. The Brothers Baldi appeared in an *Inquirer* political cartoon in 1929 (page 28).

One very parochial measure that Carmen got through the legislature was a bill that would prohibit anyone not living in its city limits to be employed by the schools or City of Philadelphia. By 1929, hundreds of such employees lived in the suburbs, so the job pool was not as controlled by the bosses as it once had been. However, fellow Republican Governor John Fisher vetoed the bill.[398]

In 1930, after his father's death, C.C.A. Baldi, Jr., inherited *L'Opinione*, and two years later, he sold it to Generoso Pope. By 1935, it had ceased to exist.[399]

Carmen's activities and community involvement were extensive as a Mason and member of the Sons of Italy in America, the Red Cross and the Salvation Army. He was also president of the Italian Federation Sons and Daughters of Columbus.[400]

Professor Varbero commented on the younger Baldi and his contemporary, the younger Di Silvestro: "In brief, neither C.C.A. Baldi, Jr., nor Anthony DiSilvestro was the peer of his immigrant father. Both younger men were successful in terms of Philadelphia politics, mainly because both had the power of organization and persuasion at their disposal. But they had inherited power; they had not created it."[401]

ROSE BALDI

Born in 1892, daughter Rose died on February 8, 1920, of what the press reported was "influenza pneumonia," the term that was used for the Spanish flu that swept the world starting in 1917, killing millions. Rose died at home at 319 Green Lane and was the first to be buried in the Baldi crypt. Shown on the following page is a photograph of her on the porch of 319 Green Lane. C.C.A.'s other daughter, Louise, named her third child Rose (later Rose Douglas Swift, Taylor Swift's grandmother).

JOSEPH F.M. BALDI, II

The fourth son born to C.C.A. and Louisa was named after Giuseppe (Joseph) Fioravanti Menotti Baldi, a brother of C.C.A. Joseph, II, was born in Philadelphia on May 11, 1894.

Rose Baldi at Green Lane. *Author's collection.*

Joseph Baldi's son Robert is a Court of Common Pleas judge in Bucks County. In a March 13, 2017, letter, he recounted:

I remember with great fondness my father telling me stories about his life and his family's life living in the house at 319 Green Lane. When I was a child, our family would drive by the house on the way to visit the Baldi burial plot located in the Westminster Cemetery and he would point the house out to us. He and my Uncle Carm (my father's brother, C.C.A. Baldi, Jr.) told my brother and me a story about one of their friends sliding on a sled down Green Lane. When they were children, the train crossed the street at the bottom of the hill. On this one particular day a boy zoomed down Green Lane as a train was slowly moving by and he went under a train car between the wheels as the train was moving forward, but fortunately timed it perfectly so that he wasn't injured or killed. They told us that the Fire Departments would test the strengths of the fire truck's engines by driving up the hill.

After graduating high school in 1912, Joseph went on to get a BS in economics from the Wharton School of Business at the University of Pennsylvania, graduating in 1916.[402]

While at the Wharton School, he became fraternity brothers with his older brother Carmen and my grandfather Charles G. Douglas. The three were in the Mu Chapter of Phi Sigma Kappa, which was a national fraternity stressing brotherhood and leadership. At the annual dinner on March 8, 1913, all three signed a leather-bound booklet with a photo

Wharton School chapter of Phi Sigma Kappa; back row, left, is Charles G. Douglas, and top right is Joe. Carmen is in the middle row, second from the right. *Author's collection.*

Left: Joseph F.M. Baldi, II, on the steps of Green Lane. *Author's collection.*

Right: Joseph Baldi on his twenty-fourth birthday, May 11, 1917, when he left for basic training. *Author's collection.*

taken of the chapter. The event was held at the Walton Hotel at Broad and Locust Streets.

In 1916, Joe began studies at the University of Pennsylvania Law School, but World War I intervened. He was a lieutenant in the 314th Infantry in France, serving until 1918. While in Europe, he had special studies in the law at the University of London and at the University of Siena in Italy.[403]

After returning from the First World War, Joe graduated from the University of Pennsylvania Law School in 1922 and set up a general practice in that year. My grandfather remained good friends with Joe.

In 1923 and 1924, Joe Baldi served as inspector of prisons for Philadelphia County. In 1927, he was selected by the Twenty-First Ward Republican leaders to run for the state legislature.[404] He served two terms, from 1929 to 1932. He also was editor of *L'Opinione* until his brother Carmen took the paper over after the death of their father in 1930.

In 1931, the *Evening Public Ledger* ran a series of interviews "with prominent bachelors of the city, telling why they have never married."[405] The article said

145

Left to right: Cheryl Baldi, Michael Alford, Meredith Baldi, David Costabile, Elizabeth Baldi Costabile and Robert O. Baldi. *Robert Baldi Collection.*

that Joe's reluctance was in part due to his experience as a divorce lawyer. "Known among his friends as one of the handsomest bachelors in the city," he had plans to never marry.[406] However, his criteria of honesty and brains was fulfilled when, at age fifty, he married Caroline Jean Otjen in 1943. In the Second World War, he served as a major in the U.S. Air Corps.

Joseph and Caroline had two sons, Joseph William Baldi (born 1946) and Robert O. Baldi (born 1949). As Rob explains:

My father married late in life. He met my mother during World War II, and they were married at the end of the war when he was 50 years old and she was 29 years old. Because my father never married until he was 50 years old, my brother Joseph and I are out of sync with our cousins. We are the closest generation to our grandfather C.C.A. Baldi.

Prior to his death at age seventy-seven in 1970 in Philadelphia, Joe was active in "civic, social, political, and charitable affairs."[407] He was a member of the Union League, American Legion, Order Sons of Italy, Italian Federation Society, Philadelphia Country Club and the Presbyterian Church.[408] His widow, Caroline, died on January 27, 2014, and she and Joseph Baldi are buried in Westminster in Bala Cynwyd across the Schuylkill River from Roxborough in the Baldi crypt.

LOUISE EURINDINE BALDI (DOUGLAS)

Born on April 26, 1896, Louise Baldi graduated from Miss Hill's School.

When she was eighteen, she was introduced to a fraternity brother of her brothers Carmen and Joseph, one Charles Gwynn Douglass. In 1914, my grandfather added an *e* to Gwynn and dropped the second *s* on Douglass. I remember my father telling me the latter change was to "take the ass out of Douglass." Thus, the wedding invitation for June 17, 1914, reads as:

Left: Wedding invitation for June 17, 1914. *Author's collection.*

Right: Louise and Charles G. Douglas. *Author's collection.*

After the wedding, my grandparents lived at 319 Green Lane for several years. At that time, women were limited in what they could do for occupations, so Louise—who was named after her mother, Louisa—threw herself into volunteer civic work.

Her lifelong love was the Presbyterian Home for the Aged in Bala Cynwyd on City Line Avenue. She rose from being a volunteer to serving as president of the board of managers for thirty-eight years. She carefully filled the board with Presbyterian stockbrokers, bankers and businessmen who helped her grow the endowment to tens of millions of dollars and expand the campus. She died on July 10, 1976, at age eighty as its honorary president.

She ran the Bala Home with a very firm hand. At some point in the 1960s, she had a falling out over policy with the trustees of the Philadelphia Presbytery. She was summoned downtown, where the assembled gentlemen threatened her with a loss of funding. She explained that would not be a problem, as she did not need, nor did she receive, funding from the Presbytery. In fact, the matter resolved when she reminded them that they received some funding from her.

The Bala Home has since been replaced by apartments, but the Bala Presbyterian Home Foundation created in 1996 provides over $1 million

Above: Louise Turner and Charles and Betsy Douglas. *Author's collection.*

Right: Louise Baldi Douglas and the author in 1943. *Author's collection.*

Opposite, left: Rose Douglas (Swift). *Author's collection.*

Opposite, right: Rose and Dean Swift during World War II. *Author's collection.*

per year for the care of elderly Presbyterians. Louise Baldi Douglas was past president of the women's board of Roxborough Memorial Hospital and a member of the Roxborough branch of the Needlework Guild and the Roxborough Visiting Nurse Society. She was a member of the First Presbyterian Church of Manayunk.

Later in life, she and her husband (who died in 1959) lived in Roxborough on Old Line Road. I knew her as "Mama-Tu."

A lifelong Republican, the only Democrat she ever voted for was Italian American Frank Rizzo for mayor. Her brother Vito's funeral home handled her husband's arrangements on his death and hers. She is buried in Plymouth Meeting, Pennsylvania.

Louise had three children: Charles G. Douglas, Jr. (1915), Emelia Louise Douglas (Turner, 1916) and Rose Baldi Douglas (Swift, 1920). Rose was my mother's roommate at Beaver College in Pennsylvania and introduced my father to Elizabeth Graham (Douglas), known as Betsy. Betsy was born and raised in Wilmington, North Carolina.

Louise Douglas married Frederick Turner, and they lived in Roxborough with their son Frederick (Rick) and daughter Joni.

Rose, known as Toni, was introduced to Archie Dean Swift, Jr., who worked with my father at Central Penn National Bank in Philadelphia.

Douglas Baldi Swift.
Author's collection.

They had three children: Archie Dean Swift, III, who died in 2014; Douglas Baldi Swift, who lives in Midland, Texas; and Scott K. Swift, who moved from near Reading, Pennsylvania, to Nashville to further the singing and songwriting career of his daughter Taylor. Scott and Andrea also have a son named Austin. (See the appendix for the Swift family line.)

Elizabeth and Charles G. Douglas, Jr., had a son, Charles, III (the author), and daughters Margaret (Frank) and Eugenia Louise (O'Brien). (See the appendix for the Douglas family line.)

VIRGIL BISMARK BALDI

The youngest child of C.C.A. Baldi was born on August 31, 1898, the year Otto Von Bismarck, the Iron Duke of Germany, died. Named after C.C.A.'s brothers Virgilio and Bismarck, Virgil was quite a traveler.

Left: Virgil B. Baldi at Green Lane. *Author's collection.*

Right: Virgil B. Baldi below a picture of his father, C.C.A., in his office in Casablanca. *Author's collection.*

In 1922, he met Ruth Mildred Johnson of Grand Forks, North Dakota, in Seattle. They married on November 6, 1924, in Minneapolis. Her father was a prominent rancher in Grand Forks. An article in the *Philadelphia Inquirer* said Virgil was chairman of the finance committee of the American Legion.[409] He grew up in Roxborough.

He served on the USS *Oklahoma* as a yeoman in the navy in World War I. At some point, he went to Europe and then moved to Casablanca in Morocco, where he lived for many years. My father said Virgil worked for the predecessor to the CIA in Morocco during World War II.

He died in Casablanca on August 17, 1960, at the age of sixty-one. He had one child, Virgil, Jr., who graduated from Haverford College and the University of Pennsylvania School of Law. Born in 1928, Virgil, Jr. was for years in the 1950s the director of personnel for Brown Raymond & Walsh, which built the American naval and air bases in Spain under President Eisenhower.

Virgil, Jr., and Janet in 1953. *Author's collection.*

Virgil, Jr., married Janet Schrauger, and they had four children: Malaga (1954), Rebecca (1958), Marta Louisa (1960) and Virgil B. Baldi, III (1961). Virgil, Jr., died in 1998 and Janet in 2015, with Virgil, III, passing in 2018. (See the appendix for the Virgil Baldi line.)

THREE SONS AT WAR

In May 1917, the Italian consul to Philadelphia, Chevalier Giovanni Gentile, was designated president of the fundraising effort of the Federated Italian Societies of Pennsylvania, New Jersey and Delaware, which had a meeting at 918 South Eighth Street in Philadelphia. The money for Italian war widows

ITALIAN ENVOYS VISIT INDEPENDENCE HALL AND HONOR HERO'S PARENTS

Italian envoys visit Independence Hall and honor hero's parents. *Author's collection.*

CHEVALIER BALDI AND HIS SOLDIER SONS

Chevalier C.C.A. Baldi (*seated*) and three of his sons, all of whom were in the military service of the United States. As they appear here, they are Lieutenant J.F.M. Baldi, Second United States Infantry, at Camp Meade, Maryland; Virgil Baldi, Naval Reserves; and Dr. Frederick S. Baldi, lieutenant in the aviation corps, stationed at League Island. *Author's collection.*

and orphans got a big kick off when Chevalier C.C.A. Baldi rose and "drew from his pockets five one-hundred-dollar bills."[410] The crowd roared, and by the end of the meeting, $2,000 had been raised.

A few days later, a goal of $100,000 was announced for the Italian Red Cross in an effort led by C.C.A.[411]

On June 22, 1917, the *Inquirer* published a photograph of dignitaries gathered to honor Mr. and Mrs. del Gatto of 764 South Eighth Street, who lost a son fighting for the Allies. Banker Edward T. Stotesbury and C.C.A. Baldi are in the front row in the top photo on page 153, to the right of Italian military officials.[412] Stotesbury's 130-room home outside Philadelphia was often compared to Versailles.

After the war's end, it was reported that the Baldi firm "had sold $600,000 worth of Liberty Bonds for the War effort."[413]

EPILOGUE

A Baldi family reunion was held at the Llanerch Country Club in Havertown, Pennsylvania, on July 8, 2016. "Cousins" from Alaska to Maine showed up for an evening of family connection all going back to several brothers who came from Castelnuovo Cilento a century and a half ago. This book is dedicated to all the Baldi and Galzerano descendants across the world.

In his doctoral dissertation for Temple University in 1975, Professor Richard Varbero well summarized C.C.A.:

> *C.C.A. Baldi responded to opportunity in American society. Both fortunate and opportunistic himself, he symbolized success to the ethnic community....*
>
> *Baldi made his own career decisions. In certain respects, the formally untrained Baldi was a Renaissance man. Unrestrained by the social barriers which would have suppressed him in tradition-ridden* bassa Italia, *Baldi succeeded in obtaining economic and political power because of his capacity to understand and deal with men of diverse cultural backgrounds. He understood Joseph Cannon, William S. Vare, and Gifford Pinchot; he understood the immigrant* contradini *as well, and the social environment which had spawned them. Honored by Italian kings and later by dictator Benito Mussolini, as well as the prestigious Manufacturers Club and the Cape May Yacht Club, Baldi lived in two worlds wresting from each the tributes to his extraordinary ambition and native intelligence. When he died on December 28, 1930, he had abandoned his Green Lane residence in*

Left: *Left to right*: Victor Baldi, III, Joe Baldi, Fred Baldi, Chuck Douglas and Rob Baldi. *Author's collection.*

Right: C.C.A. Baldi. *From Michael di Pilla*, South Philadelphia's Little Italy *(2016).*

Roxborough for the apartment over his bank on South Eighth Street. The Chevalier of the Order of Saint Maurice and Lazarus had returned to pass his last days in Little Italy. La Libera Parola, *which had often sharply disagreed with Baldi, paid him posthumous homage:*

"Conservative by conviction and temperament, he never deviated from his ethnic concepts on the essence of and the mission of the 'colony,' not even when faced by the innovative currents of the new generation. And with his tenacious and irreducible fighting temperament he confronted the tempests and passions of civic battles, without ever folding the border of his own flag."[414]

APPENDICES

FORMAZIONE DELLA LISTA DAL SINDACO   **VERIFICAZIONE**

Numero d'ordine	1. COGNOME E NOMI DELL' INSCRITTO / 2. RELIGIONE A CUI APPARTIENE	PADRE E MADRE dell'inscritto indicazione l'esistenza o la morte	NASCITA. dell' inscritto — EPOCA / 1. Giorno 2. Mese 3. Anno	LUOGO 1. Comune 2. Mandamento 3. Provincia	RESIDENZA dell'inscritto 1. Comune 2. Mandamento 3. Provincia	CONDIZIONE 1. dell'inscritto 2. di suo padre	INDICAZIONE per l'inscritto d'una classe anteriore ...	DOMANDE fatte dall'inscritto o dal padre, madre o tutore ...	VERIFICAZIONE DELLA LISTA dalla Giunta Municipale — MOTIVI delle additioni fatte alla lista ...	OSSERVAZ. sopra le domande fatte dall'inscritto o dal suo rappresentante	VERIFICAZ. definitiva DELLA LISTA — MOTIVI delle additioni, cancellazioni o correzioni fatte alla lista / ALTRE ANNOTAZ. o richiami
— 1	— 2	— 3	— 4	— 5	— 6	— 7	— 8	— 9	— 10	— 11	— 12
1	Baldi Carmine / 2 Cattolica	Vito e Catena Strago	2 Dicembre 1862	2 Valle 3							

C.C.A. Baldi's Birth Certificate.

IN THE COURT OF COMMON PLEAS

Of the County of Philadelphia, Pa.

Citizenship Application (1884).

Feb. 24, 1923

C. C. A. Baldi & Bros.
928 South Eighth Street
Philadelphia, Pa.

Gentlemen:

We have in confinement here a man who
brought with him a bank book, number
25271, on your bank issued to him under
the name of John Lavina or John Savina,
showing a deposit on September 20, 1922
of $1,000.

He desires that the money be sent to
him here. If you have a blank check
on your bank or other form of with-
drawal, if you will send it to me, I
will see that he fills it out proper-
ly and returns it to you direct or
through our bank, as you prefer.

Very truly yours,

Clerk

EAD/ARM

Di Natali

Above and opposite: 1923 Correspondence with Massachusetts Department of Corrections.

FIRST ITALIAN EXCHANGE BANK

C. C. A. BALDI & BROS.

PHILADELPHIA, PA.

CABLE
BALDIBROS

CORRESPONDENTI DEL
BANCO DI NAPOLI

March 1st, 1923.

E. A. Darling, Clerk,
Department of Correction,
State Prison,
Charlestown, Mass.

Dear Sir:-

Acknowledging yours of the 24th ult. regarding account of John Lavina beg to say we have received other instructions regarding this fund, and are waiting now to have your instructions confirmed through another source, which will be done before the end of this week, and we will at once take action.

Very truly yours,

FIRST ITALIAN EXCHANGE BANK
CHARLES C. A. BALDI & BROS.

VMB/c

Vito M Baldi

March 5, 1923

C. C. A. Baldi & Bros.
928 So. Eighth Street
Philadelphia, Pa.

Gentlemen:

I have received your letter of March 1
concerning the account of John Lavina.

You say that you "have received other
instructions regarding this fund, and
are waiting now to have your instructions confirmed through another source".
I do not understand this statement.

The man is confined here; he says that
it is his money; and nobody else has
any authority over or right to the
money.

Kindly let me know just what you mean..

Very truly yours,

Clerk

EAD/ARM

Above and opposite: 1923 Correspondence with Massachusetts Department of Corrections.

FIRST ITALIAN EXCHANGE BANK

C. C. A. BALDI & BROS.

PHILADELPHIA, PA.

CABLE
BALDIBROS

March 13th, 1923.

CORRESPONDENTI DEL
BANCO DI NAPOLI

Warden William Hendry,
Department of Correction,
State Prison,
Charlestown, Mass.

Dear Sir:-

Further acknowledging letters received from E. A. Darling, Clerk, under date of February 24th and March 5th, beg to say we have on deposit here a fund deposited in the name of John Lavina, as per the Clerk's letter of February 24th, but we had been instructed by Mr. Lavina not to withdraw under any conditions.

We, however, have completed an investigation among his friends and they take the attitude that if he wants it to send it to him.

Are we in order in asking you to inquire of the prisoner if he wants this money now on deposit? Please have him advise us the name of his father, place of birth, his age, whether single or married man, Philadelphia address, and his signature, along with an order for us to pay you the fund he has here, also enclosing his pass book.

You appreciate the position we will be placed in when Mr. Lavina is released from your custody, and we must protect ourselves this way in getting detailed information, especially when Lavina told us to hold the fund as he did when he deposited same.

Awaiting your pleasure and that of Mr. Lavina, we are

Very truly yours,

FIRST ITALIAN EXCHANGE BANK
CHARLES C. A. BALDI & BROS.

VMB/C

Vito M Baldi

163

REGIA AMBASCIATA D'ITALIA

Washington, D.C., 19 Aprile, 1907.

Egregio Signore,

A mezzo di codesto Regio Console, Cav. Fara Forni
Le perverra' la comunicazione ufficiale che la S.V. e' stata, con
recente R. Decreto, nominato Cavaliere dell'Ordine della Corona
d'Italia. Mentre sono assai compiaciuto che, in tal guisa, la
proposta a suo tempo avanzata a di Lei favore sia stata bene-
volmente accolta da S.E. il Ministro degli Affari Esteri, mi ral-
legro vivamente con Lei per la Sovrana attestazione di benemerenza
di cui Ella e' stato fatto oggetto.

Gradisca, Signor Cavaliere, gli atti della mia
distintissima considerazione.

Il Regio Ambasciatore,

E. Mayor di Planchy

Cav. C.C. Baldi

PHILADELPHIA, Pa.

C.C.A. Awarded Title of Cavaliere, April 19, 1907.

All'Ill̄mo

Sig. Cav. C. Baldi

Sonetto Acrostico.

Coll'onesto sudor della tua fronte,
Al buon voler congiunto ed all'ingegno,
Vincesti il fato, ed ascendesti il monte
A grado a grado, ove fortuna ha il regno.
L'opre tue belle, ovunque ormai ben conte,
Il tratto tuo gentil, il tuo contegno,
Le tue mani al beneficio pronte
Ti serti d'alti onori e laudi degno.
Cavalier dell'Italica Corona,
Beato or godi della sorte bella
A cui se' giunto, e che il buon Dio ti dona.
La vil caterva, che la tua grandezza
D'oscurare è bramosa, e tutta fella
Invidia a te, baldo qual sei, disprezza!

H. M. Jacobi fec.

Sonate to an Aristocrat (H. Jacobi).

TO THE MOST ILLUSTRIOUS SIR KNIGHT C. BALDI
(An Aristocratic Sonnet)

From the hard-earned perspiration of your brow,

to the combined good will and intelligence,

you defeated fate, and slowly ascended the mountain,

where fortune reigns.

Your wonderful deeds, by this time, told throughout,

your refined ways, your dignity,

and your hands, ready for kindness,

make you deserving of high honors and worthy praise.

Knight of the Italic Crown,

blessed you are, now that you enjoy the good fortune,

to which you have arrived, and that the good Lord gives you.

The unruly crowd, that your greatness is yearning to dim,

and all the cruel envy towards you, fearless that you are,

despises!

Sonate Translated into English.

C.C.A. Baldi's Death Certificate.

Baldi Brothers' Line

Vito Baldi (m. Rosa Galzerano)
(d. 1918)

C.C.A. Baldi (Carmine or Carmen)	Virgilio A. Baldi	Giuseppe (Joseph) Fioravanti Baldi	Guerino Carmelo (William) Baldi	Alfonso L. (Antonio) Baldi	Grace or Grazia Bald
b. 12-2-1862 1876 to Phila.	b. 11-28-1864	b. 2-16-1870	b. 1-02-1875 d. 6-25-1909	b. 2-22-1886	m. Peter Jacovini 1906
adds "Charles" to his name in U.S.	d. 1957 at age 93 according to Victor Baldi, III		m. Bessie L. Cowperthwaite 2-24-1905	(see Al and Fred lines)	
d. 12-30-30	buried in Baldi Crypt				
m. Louisa Sobernheimer 1886 (d. 3-20-24)					

Joseph Baldi Line

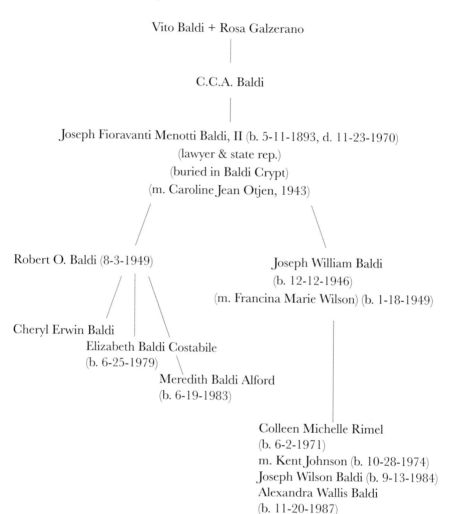

Vito Baldi + Rosa Galzerano

C.C.A. Baldi

Joseph Fioravanti Menotti Baldi, II (b. 5-11-1893, d. 11-23-1970)
(lawyer & state rep.)
(buried in Baldi Crypt)
(m. Caroline Jean Otjen, 1943)

Robert O. Baldi (8-3-1949)

Joseph William Baldi
(b. 12-12-1946)
(m. Francina Marie Wilson) (b. 1-18-1949)

Cheryl Erwin Baldi
Elizabeth Baldi Costabile
(b. 6-25-1979)

Meredith Baldi Alford
(b. 6-19-1983)

Colleen Michelle Rimel
(b. 6-2-1971)
m. Kent Johnson (b. 10-28-1974)
Joseph Wilson Baldi (b. 9-13-1984)
Alexandra Wallis Baldi
(b. 11-20-1987)

VIRGIL BALDI LINE

Vito Baldi & Rosa Galzerano

Charles Carmen Antonio Baldi
(m. Louisa Sobernheimer)
b. 12-2-1862
d. 12-28-1930

Virgil Bismark Baldi
b. 8-31-1898
(m. Ruth Johnson)

Virgil B. Baldi, Jr. (b. 1-2-1928, d. 6-98) m. Janet Shrauger (b. 2-1-1930, d. 11-6-2015)

Malaga Baldi (b. 1954)
(m. Lucy Painter)

Rebecca Baldi (b. 1958)
(m. Denis A. Assad) (b. 1956)

Marta Luisa Baldi (b. 1960)   Virgil B. Baldi, III (b. 1961)
(m. Arthur Mark Schaffer)   (d. 1-26-2018)

Orian Baldi Painter
(b. 1996)
                              Susan Schaffer (b. 1980)
                                 (m. Anthony Brown) (b. 1982)
                              Rebecca Lynn Schaffer (b. 1986)
                              Jacqueline Schaffer (b. 1988)
                                 (m. Matthew Justin Sundheim)

BALDI/SWIFT LINE

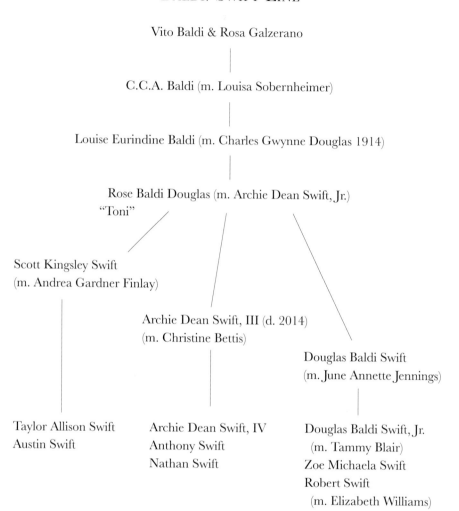

Vito Baldi & Rosa Galzerano

C.C.A. Baldi (m. Louisa Sobernheimer)

Louise Eurindine Baldi (m. Charles Gwynne Douglas 1914)

Rose Baldi Douglas (m. Archie Dean Swift, Jr.)
"Toni"

Scott Kingsley Swift
(m. Andrea Gardner Finlay)

Archie Dean Swift, III (d. 2014)
(m. Christine Bettis)

Douglas Baldi Swift
(m. June Annette Jennings)

Taylor Allison Swift
Austin Swift

Archie Dean Swift, IV
Anthony Swift
Nathan Swift

Douglas Baldi Swift, Jr.
(m. Tammy Blair)
Zoe Michaela Swift
Robert Swift
(m. Elizabeth Williams)

DOUGLAS LINE FROM C.C.A. BALDI

Vito Baldi married Rosa Galzerano

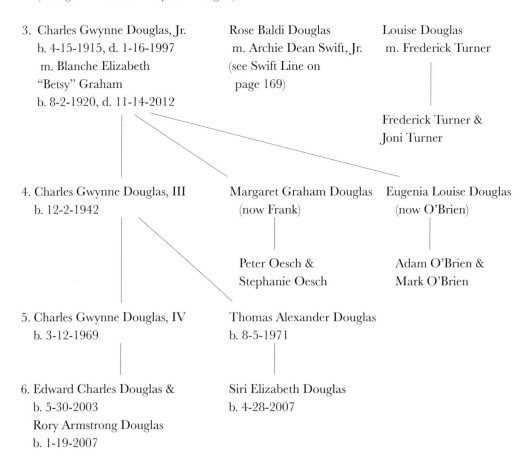

1. Charles Carmen Antonio Baldi
   b. 12-2-1862 as Carmine
   m. Louisa E. Sobernheimer 1886

2. Louise Eurindine Baldi
   b. 4-26-1896
   m. Charles Gwynn Douglass 1914
   (changed to Charles Gwynne Douglas)

3. Charles Gwynne Douglas, Jr.
   b. 4-15-1915, d. 1-16-1997
   m. Blanche Elizabeth
   "Betsy" Graham
   b. 8-2-1920, d. 11-14-2012

   Rose Baldi Douglas
   m. Archie Dean Swift, Jr.
   (see Swift Line on
   page 169)

   Louise Douglas
   m. Frederick Turner

   Frederick Turner &
   Joni Turner

4. Charles Gwynne Douglas, III
   b. 12-2-1942

   Margaret Graham Douglas
   (now Frank)

   Peter Oesch &
   Stephanie Oesch

   Eugenia Louise Douglas
   (now O'Brien)

   Adam O'Brien &
   Mark O'Brien

5. Charles Gwynne Douglas, IV
   b. 3-12-1969

   Thomas Alexander Douglas
   b. 8-5-1971

6. Edward Charles Douglas &
   b. 5-30-2003
   Rory Armstrong Douglas
   b. 1-19-2007

   Siri Elizabeth Douglas
   b. 4-28-2007

FRED BALDI LINE

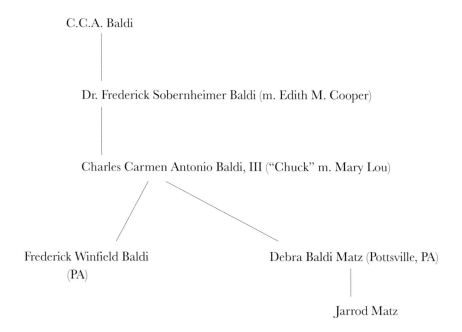

C.C.A. Baldi

Dr. Frederick Sobernheimer Baldi (m. Edith M. Cooper)

Charles Carmen Antonio Baldi, III ("Chuck" m. Mary Lou)

Frederick Winfield Baldi (PA)

Debra Baldi Matz (Pottsville, PA)

Jarrod Matz

ALFONSO LUIGI BALDI LINE

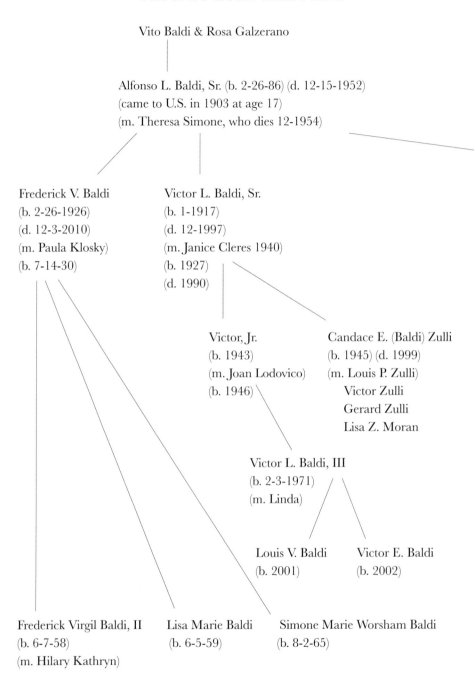

Vito Baldi & Rosa Galzerano

Alfonso L. Baldi, Sr. (b. 2-26-86) (d. 12-15-1952)
(came to U.S. in 1903 at age 17)
(m. Theresa Simone, who dies 12-1954)

Frederick V. Baldi
(b. 2-26-1926)
(d. 12-3-2010)
(m. Paula Klosky)
(b. 7-14-30)

Victor L. Baldi, Sr.
(b. 1-1917)
(d. 12-1997)
(m. Janice Cleres 1940)
(b. 1927)
(d. 1990)

Victor, Jr.
(b. 1943)
(m. Joan Lodovico)
(b. 1946)

Candace E. (Baldi) Zulli
(b. 1945) (d. 1999)
(m. Louis P. Zulli)
Victor Zulli
Gerard Zulli
Lisa Z. Moran

Victor L. Baldi, III
(b. 2-3-1971)
(m. Linda)

Louis V. Baldi
(b. 2001)

Victor E. Baldi
(b. 2002)

Frederick Virgil Baldi, II
(b. 6-7-58)
(m. Hilary Kathryn)

Lisa Marie Baldi
(b. 6-5-59)

Simone Marie Worsham Baldi
(b. 8-2-65)

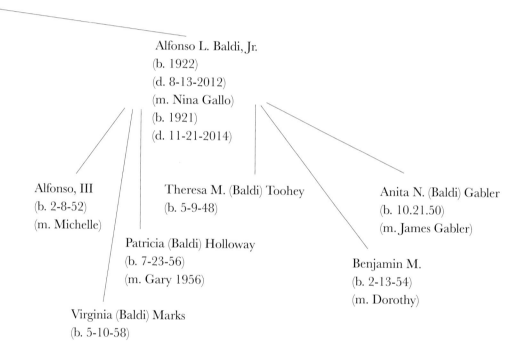

Alfonso L. Baldi, Jr.
(b. 1922)
(d. 8-13-2012)
(m. Nina Gallo)
(b. 1921)
(d. 11-21-2014)

Alfonso, III
(b. 2-8-52)
(m. Michelle)

Theresa M. (Baldi) Toohey
(b. 5-9-48)

Anita N. (Baldi) Gabler
(b. 10.21.50)
(m. James Gabler)

Patricia (Baldi) Holloway
(b. 7-23-56)
(m. Gary 1956)

Benjamin M.
(b. 2-13-54)
(m. Dorothy)

Virginia (Baldi) Marks
(b. 5-10-58)

NOTES

Chapter 1

1. Stefano Luconi, *From Paesani to White Ethnics* (Albany: State University of New York Press, 2001), 35.
2. Richard A. Varbero, "Urbanization and Acculturation: Philadelphia's South Italians," PhD diss., Temple University, 1975, 39.
3. Ibid., 42.
4. Michael Di Pilla, *South Philadelphia's Little Italy and 9ᵗʰ Street Italian Market* (Charleston, SC: Arcadia Publishing, 2016), 9.

Chapter 2

5. Stefano Luconi, Encyclopedia of Greater Philadelphia, essay on Italians, 1.
6. Ibid., 2.
7. Ibid.
8. Ibid.
9. Ibid.
10. Ibid.
11. Ibid.
12. Ibid.
13. Ibid.
14. Ibid.

15. Di Pilla, *South Philadelphia's Little Italy*, 9.
16. Luconi, Encyclopedia of Greater Philadelphia, fn. 1, 3.
17. Ibid.

Chapter 3

18. *Reading Times*, March 10, 1919, 2.
19. Varbero, "Urbanization and Acculturation," fn. 2, 284.
20. *Evening Public Ledger*, June 29, 1915, 6.

Chapter 4

21. Luconi, Encyclopedia of Greater Philadelphia, chapter on Italians, 4.
22. Varbero, "Urbanization and Acculturation," fn. 2, 141.
23. Ibid., 142.
24. Ibid., 145.
25. Ibid., 144.
26. Ibid., 149.

Chapter 5

27. *Philadelphia Inquirer*, January 20, 1917, 10.
28. Ibid., February 16, 1928, 9.
29. *Reading Eagle*, December 3, 1936.

Chapter 6

30. *Philadelphia Inquirer*, March 2, 1924, 2.
31. Ibid.
32. Ibid., March 27, 1910, 8.
33. Ibid., April 3, 1910, 8.
34. *Evening Public Ledger*, January 8, 1920, 11.
35. *Washington Post*, January 9, 1913.
36. *Philadelphia Inquirer*, January 9, 1913, 4.
37. Ibid.

Chapter 7

38. *Philadelphia Inquirer*, June 17, 1909, 1.
39. *Asbury Park Press*, May 17, 1911, 6.
40. *Philadelphia Inquirer*, June 1, 1911, 4.
41. *Evening Public Ledger*, March 3, 1915, 2.
42. *Bristol Daily Courier*, February 22, 1927.
43. Luconi, *From Paesani to White Ethnics.*
44. *Philadelphia Inquirer*, May 21, 1909, 11.
45. Ibid., August 19, 1918, 5.
46. Ibid.
47. Ibid., October 2, 1920, 6.
48. Ibid., November 22, 1925, 92.
49. *Newark Jewish Chronicle*, June 22, 1928, 10.
50. Luconi, *From Paesani to White Ethnics*, 19.
51. *Philadelphia Inquirer*, September 13, 1914.
52. *Evening Public Ledger*, 1923.
53. *Philadelphia Inquirer*, June 28, 1909, 7.

Chapter 8

54. *Evening Public Ledger*, June 29, 1915, 6.
55. *Philadelphia Inquirer*, March 8, 1905.
56. Samuel Hudson, *Pennsylvania and Its Public Men* (n.p., 1907), 298.
57. A. Frangini, *Italiani in Filadelfia* (n.p., 1907).
58. *Philadelphia Inquirer*, January 7, 1909, 14.
59. *Harrisburg Evening News*, May 12, 1925, 6.
60. *Indiana Gazette*, May 12, 1925, 12.
61. *Pittsburgh Daily Post*, May 14, 1925, 5.
62. *Harrisburg Telegram*, November 14, 1925, 10.
63. *L'Opinione*, January 14, 1931, 1.

Chapter 9

64. Di Pilla, *South Philadelphia's Little Italy*, 63.
65. Ibid.
66. Ibid.

67. Varbero, "Urbanization and Acculturation," fn. 2, 145.
68. Di Pilla, *South Philadelphia's Little Italy*, 63.
69. Ibid.
70. Ibid., 70.
71. Ibid.
72. Hudson, *Pennsylvania and Its Public Men*, 298.
73. Varbero, "Urbanization and Acculturation," fn. 2, 151.
74. Ibid., 147–48.
75. *Delaware County Daily Times*, January 6, 1931.
76. *San Diego Evening Tribune*, January 6, 1931, 26.
77. *Delaware County Daily Times*, January 6, 1931.

Chapter 10

78. Stefano Luconi, "The Changing Meaning of Ethnic Identity among Italian Americans in Philadelphia during the Interwar Years," *Pennsylvania Magazine of History and Biography* 63 (Autumn 1996): 562.
79. Ibid.
80. Ibid.
81. Ibid.
82. Ibid., 563.
83. Ibid., 564.
84. Ibid.
85. Ibid.
86. Varbero, "Urbanization and Acculturation," fn. 2, 304.
87. Ibid., 305.
88. Luconi, "Changing Meaning of Ethnic Identity," fn. 78, 564.
89. Ibid., 565.
90. Ibid.
91. Ibid.
92. Ibid.
93. Ibid., 566.
94. Ibid., 567.
95. Luconi, *From Paesani to White Ethnics*, 33.
96. Luconi, "Changing Meaning of Ethnic Identity," fn. 78, 567.
97. R.M. MacIver, ed., *Group Relations and Group Antagonisms* (New York: Harper and Brothers, 1944): 32.
98. Luconi, *From Paesani to White Ethnics*, 33.

99. Ibid., 34.
100. Ibid.
101. Ibid.
102. Ibid.
103. Ibid.
104. Ibid.
105. Ibid.
106. Ibid.
107. Ibid.
108. Ibid., 35.
109. Ibid.
110. Ibid.
111. Varbero, "Urbanization and Acculturation," fn. 2, 303.
112. Ibid., 306.
113. Ibid., 308–9.
114. Ibid., 308.
115. Ibid., 309.
116. Ibid.
117. Luconi, *From Paesani to White Ethnics*, 80.
118. Ibid.
119. Ibid.
120. Ibid.
121. Ibid.

Chapter 11

122. Caroline Golab, *Immigrant Destinations* (Philadelphia: Temple University Press, 1977), 214.
123. Ibid.
124. Ibid.
125. Ibid.
126. Ibid.
127. Ibid.
128. Ibid.
129. Ibid.
130. Ibid.
131. *Philadelphia Inquirer*, December 14, 1907, 1.
132. Ibid.

133. Ibid.

134. Ibid., October 27, 1913, 2.

135. Luconi, "Changing Meaning of Ethnic Identity," 568.

136. *Philadelphia Inquirer*, July 30, 1919, 12.

137. *Trenton Evening Times*, January 25, 1908.

138. *Philadelphia Inquirer*, October 27, 1919, 2.

139. Ibid.

140. Golab, *Immigrant Destinations*, fn. 1, 215.

141. Ibid.

142. Ibid.

143. *Philadelphia Inquirer*, May 28, 1909, 4.

144. Ibid.

145. Ibid.

146. Ibid., September 9, 1910, 2.

147. Ibid.

148. Ibid.

149. Ibid., September 10, 1910, 1.

150. "Detained Aliens Secure Freedom," *Philadelphia Inquirer*, September 17, 1910, 6.

151. "Save Six Italians from Deportation," *Philadelphia Inquirer*, September 29, 1910, 8.

152. Ibid.

153. *Wilmington (DE) Evening Journal*, September 29, 1910, 7.

154. *Philadelphia Inquirer*, February 7, 1913, 16.

155. Ibid.

156. Ibid., February 21, 1924, 6.

157. Ibid.

Chapter 12

158. *Wall Street Journal*, October 10, 2009, 1.

159. Luconi, *From Paesani to White Ethnics*, 35.

160. Ibid.

161. *Philadelphia Inquirer*, July 22, 1902.

162. Ibid.

163. Ibid., February 24, 1909, 6.

164. Ibid., October 3, 1910, 6.

165. Ibid.

166. *Baltimore Sun*, August 16, 1921, 5.

167. *Philadelphia Inquirer*, July 18, 1908, 2.

168. Ibid.

169. Ibid.

170. Ibid.

171. Ibid., June 21, 1917, 2.

172. Luconi, *From Paesani to White Ethnics*, fn. 2, 36.

173. Ibid.

174. Ibid., 37.

175. *Philadelphia Inquirer*, May 3, 1912, 2.

176. Ibid.

177. Ibid., September 2, 1915, 2.

178. Ibid.

179. Ibid., January 14, 1916, 6.

180. Ibid., February 20, 1916, 2.

181. *Pittsburgh Post-Gazette*, February 25, 1919, 8.

182. Ibid.

183. Ibid.

184. Ibid.

185. *Harrisburg Telegram*, March 11, 1919, 5.

186. Ibid.

187. *Philadelphia Inquirer*, December 17, 1919, 12.

188. Ibid.

189. Ibid.

190. Ibid., March 4, 1920, 2.

191. Ibid., March 15, 1920, 8.

192. Ibid.

193. Ibid., March 4, 1920, 2.

194. Ibid., March 15, 1920, 8.

195. Ibid.

196. *Baltimore Sun*, August 16, 1921, 5.

197. Suzanna Rosa Molino, *Baltimore's Little Italy: Heritage and History of the Neighborhood* (Charleston, SC: The History Press, 2015), 103.

Chapter 13

198. *Evening Public Ledger*, June 29, 1915, 6.

199. "Little Italians Win Prizes," *Philadelphia Inquirer*, June 19, 1901.

200. *Philadelphia Inquirer*, October 27, 1901, 20.

201. Ibid., January 23, 1911, 11.

202. Ibid., October 4, 1924, 16.

203. Ibid., October 15, 1924, 2.

204. Ibid., May 7, 1925, 11.

205. Ibid.

206. Ibid., May 17, 1925, 87.

207. Ibid., May 19, 1925, editorial page.

208. Ibid., April 27, 1910, 4.

209. Ibid., January 23, 1911, 11.

210. Ibid.

211. Ibid., March 14, 1911, 8.

212. *Bristol Daily Courier*, April 21, 1911, 1.

213. *Philadelphia Inquirer*, October 31, 1915, 3.

214. *Wilmington News Journal*, October 11, 1919, 3.

215. *Wilmington Morning News*, August 3, 1920, 1.

216. Ibid.

217. *Wilmington News Journal*, August 3, 1920, 14.

218. *Philadelphia Inquirer*, February 28, 1927, 5.

Chapter 14

219. Frangini, *Italiani in Filadelfia*, 5.

220. *Central News*, September 4, 1902, 1.

221. *Philadelphia Inquirer*, September 1, 1902, 9.

222. Ibid., August 27, 1902, 2.

223. Ibid., September 27, 1902.

224. Ibid., July 29, 1903, 1.

225. Ibid.

226. Ibid., July 28, 1903, 11.

227. Ibid., September 19, 1905, 7.

228. Ibid. The carriages were likely those owned by the Baldi funeral home.

229. *Carlisle Evening Herald*, May 18, 1907, 2.

230. *Anniston Star*, October 1, 1926, 5.

231. *Philadelphia Inquirer*, June 3, 1907.

232. Ibid., October 17, 1907, 9.

233. Ibid.

234. Ibid., July 6, 1908, 8.

235. Ibid., November 17, 1908, 11.

236. Ibid.

237. Ibid., November 29, 1908, 28.

238. *Altoona Tribune*, December 30, 1908, 4.

239. *Philadelphia Inquirer*, December 21, 1908, 1.

240. Ibid., January 4, 1908, 2.

241. Ibid., December 30, 1908, 2.

242. Ibid., January 5, 1909, 2.

243. Ibid., October 27, 1908, 4.

244. Ibid., June 9, 1916, 10.

245. Ibid., August 15, 2016, 10.

246. Ibid., December 4, 2016, 13.

247. Ibid.

248. Ibid., November 2, 1929, 8.

249. Ibid., July 18, 1926.

250. Ibid.

251. *Reading Times*, December 19, 1902, 1.

252. Ibid., December 20, 1902, 2.

253. Ibid.

254. *Philadelphia Inquirer*, July 15, 1915, 5.

255. Ibid., August 6, 1915, 11.

256. Ibid., November 8, 1908, 1.

257. Ibid., April 26, 1907.

258. Ibid., May 31, 1907, 2.

259. Ibid., December 23, 1919, 9.

Chapter 15

260. William S. Vare, *My Forty Years in Politics* (Philadelphia: Roland Swain Company, 1933), 80–81.

261. John M. Barry, *The Great Influenza: The Story of the Deadliest Pandemic in History* (New York: Penguin, 2005), 198.

262. Stefano Luconi, "Bringing Out the Italian-American Vote in Philadelphia," *Pennsylvania Magazine of History and Biography* (October 1993): 264.

263. Barry, *Great Influenza*, fn. 2, 199.

264. Ibid.

265. Luconi, *From Paesani to White Ethnics*, 60.

266. *Philadelphia Inquirer*, September 23, 1911, 2.

267. Ibid.
268. Varbero, "Urbanization and Acculturation," 289, 290.
269. John Thomas Salter, *Boss Rule: Portraits in City Politics* (n.p., 1955), 30.
270. Varbero, "Urbanization and Acculturation," fn. 2, 292.
271. Ibid., 286.
272. Luconi, "Changing Meaning of Ethnic Identity," 563.
273. Varbero, "Urbanization and Acculturation," fn. 2, 333.
274. Ibid., 348.
275. Ibid., 364.
276. Ibid., 349.
277. Ibid.
278. Ibid., 350.
279. Ibid., 355.
280. Ibid., 357.
281. Ibid., 364.
282. Ibid., 366.
283. Ibid.
284. Ibid., 367.

Chapter 16

285. Varbero, "Urbanization and Acculturation," fn. 2, 290.
286. Ibid., 291.
287. Ibid., 294, 296.
288. Ibid., 306.
289. Ibid., 307.
290. Ibid., 308.
291. Luconi, *From Paesani to White Ethnics*, 80.
292. Ibid.
293. Ibid., 37.
294. Varbero, "Urbanization and Acculturation," fn. 2, 309.
295. Ibid., 308.
296. *Philadelphia Inquirer*, December 29, 1930, 4.
297. Luconi, *From Paesani to White Ethnics*, 37.
298. *Momento* (Philadelphia), June 23, 1917, 3.
299. *Evening Public Ledger*, June 25, 1917, 2.
300. Ibid.
301. Ibid.

302. *Philadelphia Inquirer*, July 3, 1917, 6.

303. Ibid.

304. Ibid.

305. Ibid., July 9, 1917, 6.

306. *Evening Public Ledger*, August 11, 1917, 3.

307. Ibid.

308. Philip M. Rose, *The Italians in America* (New York: George H. Doran Company, 1922), 82. The factionalism in the Italian community in Philadelphia is evident in newspaper accounts of the period. See, for example, "Italians at Meeting Repudiate Bossism," *Philadelphia Public Ledger*, October 5, 1917, 3.

309. Luconi, "Changing Meaning of Ethnic Identity," 571–72.

310. Ibid., 572.

311. *Public Ledger*, December 29, 1930, 1.

Chapter 17

312. *Philadelphia Inquirer*, May 30, 1904, 1.

313. Ibid.

314. Ibid.

315. Ibid.

316. Ibid., October 10, 1921, 10.

317. Ibid.

318. Ibid.

319. Ibid.

320. Ibid.

321. Ibid., March 27, 1922, 6.

322. Ibid., April 4, 1924, 2.

323. *Vancouver Daily World*, May 4, 1923, 11.

324. *Philadelphia Inquirer*, April 22, 1923, 1.

325. Ibid.

326. *Lebanon (PA) Evening Reporter*, April 21, 1923.

327. *Harrisburg Evening News*, April 21, 1923, 12.

328. *New Castle Herald*, April 21, 1923, 1.

329. Ibid., April 21, 1923, 2.

330. *Philadelphia Inquirer*, July 4, 1923, 6.

331. Ibid., May 11, 1923, 2.

332. Ibid.

333. *Bristol Daily Courier*, November 24, 1923, 1.

334. *Altoona Tribune*, November 28, 1923, 11.

335. *Harrisburg Evening News*, November 26, 1923.

336. *Philadelphia Inquirer*, November 25, 1923, 4.

337. *Pittsburgh Daily Post*, June 20, 1927, 2.

338. Ibid.

339. Luconi, "Changing Meaning of Ethnic Identity," 566.

Chapter 19

340. *Public Ledger*, March 29, 1930, 1.

341. Relayed to the author by his father many decades ago.

342. *Public Ledger*, December 29, 1930, 1.

343. Ibid.

344. *Suburban Press*, January 8, 1931, 1.

345. Ibid.

346. Ibid.

347. Ibid.

348. Ibid.

349. Ibid., 5.

350. *Catholic Advance*, January 17, 1931, 6.

351. *Delaware County Daily Times*, December 29, 1930.

352. *Suburban Press*, January 8, 1931, 5.

353. Ibid.

Chapter 20

354. *Philadelphia Inquirer*, May 7, 1905.

355. Ibid.

356. Frederick S. Baldi, *My Unwelcome Guests* (Philadelphia: J.B. Lippincott Company, 1959), 32.

357. *Philadelphia Inquirer*, June 12, 1910, 6.

358. Baldi, *My Unwelcome Guests*, fn. 357, 15.

359. Ibid., 16.

360. *Philadelphia Inquirer*, June 12, 1910, 6.

361. Ibid.

362. Charles Baldi, *Hucksters and Horses* (2007), 246–50.

363. *Philadelphia Inquirer*, July 23, 1910, 7.

364. Ibid., June 13, 1913, 2.

365. Baldi, *My Unwelcome Guests*, fn. 357, 33.

366. Ibid., 18.

367. Ibid., 108.

368. Ibid., 122.

369. Ibid., 109.

370. Ibid.

371. Ibid.

372. Ibid., 21.

373. Ibid., 22.

374. Ibid.

375. Ibid., 23.

376. Ibid.

377. Ibid., 24.

378. Varbero, "Urbanization and Acculturation," fn. 2, 306.

379. Joseph William Carlevale, *Americans of Italian Descent in Philadelphia* (Philadelphia: George S. Ferguson Co., 1950), 22–23.

380. *Philadelphia Inquirer*, June 21, 1910, 14.

381. Carlevale, *Americans of Italian Descent*, 21.

382. *Pittsburgh Press*, July 5, 1916, 22.

383. Ibid., September 14, 1916, 11.

384. Ibid.

385. *Philadelphia Inquirer*, September 15, 1916, 8.

386. *Reading Times*, September 16, 1916, 5.

387. Ibid.

388. *Philadelphia Inquirer*, April 15, 1917, 2.

389. Ibid., October 6, 1916, 1.

390. Ibid., November 8, 1916, 14.

391. George P. Donehoo, ed., *Pennsylvania: A History* (n.p.: Lewis Historical, 1926), 165.

392. Ibid.

393. Ibid.

394. *Scranton Republican*, March 12, 1919, 12.

395. *Philadelphia Inquirer*, April 23, 1919, 5.

396. *News Journal*, April 7, 1927, 18.

397. Varbero, "Urbanization and Acculturation," fn. 2, 368.

398. *Evening News*, May 1, 1929, 22.

399. Luconi, *From Paesani to White Ethnics*, 80.

400. Carlevale, *Americans of Italian Descent*, 22.

401. Varbero, "Urbanization and Acculturation," fn. 2, 369.

402. Your author attended Wharton part time in 1963.

403. Varbero, "Urbanization and Acculturation," fn. 2, 22.

404. *Philadelphia Inquirer*, February 25, 1927, 2.

405. *Evening Public Ledger,* July 24, 1931.

406. Ibid.

407. Varbero, "Urbanization and Acculturation," fn. 2, 22.

408. Ibid.

409. *Philadelphia Inquirer*, November 29, 1924, 20.

410. *Evening Public Ledger*, May 30, 1917, 7.

411. *Philadelphia Inquirer,* June 3, 1917, 2.

412. Ibid., June 22, 1917, 2. Stotesbury made his millions in banking, and his home named Whitemarsh Hall had 140 rooms on three hundred acres outside Philadelphia in Wyndmoor.

413. *Evening Public Ledger*, December 18, 1918, 10.

Epilogue

414. Varbero, "Urbanization and Acculturation," fn. 2, 287–88.

ABOUT THE AUTHOR

harles G. Douglas, III, was born in Abington, Pennsylvania, on December 2, 1942, which is the same day C.C.A. Baldi was born eighty years earlier. Chuck grew up on a farm in Jarrettown near Fort Washington and graduated from Penn Charter School in Germantown in 1960. Two years later, the family moved to New Hampshire, and Chuck graduated from the University of New Hampshire and then got his law degree from Boston University in 1968.

He served as legal counsel to the governor from 1973 to 1974, when he became a judge on the Superior Court. In 1977, he became a justice on the New Hampshire Supreme Court, where he served until 1985.

He is the author of two other books on evidence and family law and is a trial attorney with his own law firm in Concord, New Hampshire. Chuck served in the New Hampshire Army National Guard for twenty-three years before retiring as a colonel.

He and his wife, Debra, live in Bow, New Hampshire, where they serve as publisher and editors of the *Bow Times*, the local newspaper, with a circulation of 4,100. Debra also chairs the New Hampshire Lottery Commission.

One of his sons lives just outside Philadelphia and the other in Alaska.

Stories from Chuck's father about C.C.A. were the motivating factor in writing this book so he could share an exciting life well lived.

Visit us at
www.historypress.com
·······································